The Presence of the Soul

The Presence of the Soul

Transforming Your Life
through
Soul Awareness

John L. Payne

First published by Findhorn Press 2007

ISBN: 978-1-84409-115-7

British Library Cataloguing-in-Publication Data.
A catalogue record for this book is available from the British Library.

Edited by Jean Semrau
Cover design by Damian Keenan
Layout by Pam Bochel
Printed and bound by WS Bookwell, Finland

1 2 3 4 5 6 7 8 9 10 11 12 13 12 11 10 09 08 07

Published by
Findhorn Press
305A The Park,
Findhorn, Forres
Scotland IV36 3TE

Tel 01309 690582
Fax 01309 690036
email: info@findhornpress.com
www.findhornpress.com

TABLE OF CONTENTS

Prologue – Self-Image and the Soul   1

Introduction – Expression of the Soul   16

Chapter One – The World Is What It Is   26

Chapter Two – The Burdens of Guilt and Remorse   39

Chapter Three – Uncovering Hidden Loyalties   46

Chapter Four – Inherited Belief Systems   65

Chapter Five – Discovering Essence   76

Chapter Six – Experiencing the Presence of the Soul   93

Chapter Seven – Becoming Conscious of What You Want   105

Chapter Eight – Getting There from Here   115

Chapter Nine – The Power of Gratitude   133

Chapter Ten – Self-Appreciation   138

Chapter Eleven – Spiritual Practice   145

Chapter Twelve – Reincarnation   148

Final Chapter – Key Points   159

About the Author   165

Acknowledgements

As with many journeys, and certainly a journey through life experience, I have not made this journey alone and would like to thank some of my companions: Thierry Bogliolo for his continued support for my work and my writing, and the staff at Findhorn Press that have assisted with this process: Jean Semrau, Alyssa Bonilla, Carol Shaw and many others. To my dear friend Hilda de la Rosa for her honesty, clarity of thought and good advice; Carol Kulig for holding my hand at times when I questioned my whole journey and my worthiness for doing this work; Annebiene Pilon for being such a guiding light in my life; Gerrit Koelers for making me laugh so often; Will and Lynn Mitchell in Scotland for their generosity; Bud Weiss, Tuck Self and Maggie Self for their enthusiastic support of my work; and also Sandi Bingel and Margie Pretorius in Kwa-Zulu Natal for their selfless service to my work – thank you! I would also like to thank Laura Santoni-Wing and Pat Bastani in Cape Town; Svenja Wachter; Shahzaad Hones and her husband; Colleen Ballenden; Marian Bourne and many others for their support. A special mention must go to Philip Johnson, a trusted and respected Tai Chi instructor and Healing Tao practitioner of note, and to my friends Darlene Smith and Di du Preez for their love and support. The presence of all these people's souls has touched my life immeasurably.

A special thank you to Larry Reed, Nancy Mayans, Fortunee Dank and Barney Stein for their friendship and support, and to Rosinha Zuwalu, my housekeeper, without whom my books would never get written on time!

A thank you must also go to my dear friend Sam Weber and to Willie Engelbrecht. In your deaths, you gave me gifts I cannot measure. Please wait patiently for me, I shall come when it is my proper time. Until then, happy journeys!

Lastly, a big thank you must be given to the entire nation of South Africa. Living in this nation has brought me knowledge, experience and growth that I truly could not have gained in any other country. It is my deepest wish that the cycle of victims and perpetrators may soon come to a peaceful end within the heart of South Africa.

Nkosi sikelel' iAfrika.

(God bless Africa.)

PROLOGUE

SELF-IMAGE AND THE SOUL

Distorted self-images are probably the greatest block we have to the presence of our own soul. The events and circumstances, and how adults spoke to us as we grew up, led us to form many beliefs about ourselves and the world, many of them becoming almost set in concrete until the day we make the decision to examine our lives, not out of blame for others, but out of our desire to reach for something better. What is very clear about negative self- images and limiting belief systems is that they did not start with our parents, for they were just as subject to these as we were. Just like genes and chromosomes, beliefs, shame and trauma are also passed down from one generation to the next, and they continue to be passed down until someone makes the decision to break the chain and re-start life with a different set of beliefs.

When I was growing up, I was subject to much physical violence at the hands of a family member. He would get into rages with little to no provocation and I would often find myself the object of that uncontrolled rage. However, despite trying to communicate what was going on to my parents, my pleas for help went unheard, and this later turned into sexual abuse and the blackmail that went with it. This all happened when I was between the ages of eleven and fifteen and my life was at a low ebb, which is quite a statement to be making about a young teenager. I took on the belief that I was in some way unimportant, not loved, and I ended up feeling guilty for my own suffering, believing that I was just a "cry baby", as I had once been told. At this young age I began to see the world as an unsafe place; a world in which there was no haven for the young; a world in which few people, if any, cared what happened to others. This belief led to the creation of a blueprint upon which I would build my life in later years. Control and an attempt to dominate became regular themes.

In an effort to escape my misery I turned to religion, first as an altar boy at the local Catholic church – but that was very short-lived as I was constantly being chastised for asking too many probing questions about religion, God and the nature of life. The belief that I did not matter continued and deepened. I remember going to confession and starting with the usual, "Bless me Father, for I have sinned", and then going silent; I could think of nothing wrong that I had done. I was the typical angelic child and the only thing I had ever done wrong in my life was to steal some pencils from a shop as a dare with a group of friends. I quietly said to my priest that I hadn't sinned that week. What I got in response was a raised voice and fifty Our Fathers and fifty Hail Marys for being haughty and for blasphemy. I was asked to leave my position as altar boy within days of that experience. This left me feeling that, no matter how "good" I was, I was still "bad" in someone's eyes, especially in the eyes of God.

Some time later, two very friendly women came to the door of our home during the school holidays. I was fourteen and home alone at the time. They wanted to speak about God and I listened to them for about an hour. Everything they told me was like music to my ears. Their message was that God's Kingdom would soon be established on earth, all evil would come to an end, and humanity would live in peace. The message was very appealing. All I needed to do was believe in their religion and I would be safe from the ravages of God's wrath. As my life was so miserable, the notion of being saved from wrath and preserved in a world of "good" people was something that I definitely wanted. The two ladies were Jehovah's Witnesses and I spent the next four years going to their meetings, in secret at first. Their religion seemed to offer me a way out of my misery and I was ready to vote for any religion that promised me paradise.

A few short weeks after I met these two women, however, my father told me that we would be moving from Australia back to England and that we would be leaving in a couple of weeks' time. I was devastated. I was actively involved in horse riding and was about to acquire my first horse which was a gift from an elderly gentleman who had befriended me during my newspaper rounds at the local hospital. I could not believe that what little happiness I had was going to be ripped away from me. Again, it seemed as if I was not important and that I was invisible. My feeling that the world was unsafe simply deepened, for it seemed that my world could be changed or ripped away from me at the whim of an adult and that I had no say whatsoever. I had been invisible to the Catholic Church, my beatings at the hands of another were also somehow totally invisible to my parents, and now, with no consultation or consideration, the one thing I loved was being taken away from me. In my eyes, I was invisible, I did not matter, I was not important, and therefore I began to believe that I was neither loved nor cared for in any great measure and that, ultimately, I was unsafe. I simply could not trust the adults around me to care for my needs.

When we moved to England the brother who had terrorized me when we lived in Australia became worse in his behaviour and he attempted suicide on a couple of occasions. He was placed in a psychiatric hospital, for he was struggling with depression and anorexia; later he was diagnosed with schizophrenia. For me, it was a relief that he was elsewhere. It seemed to me that the entire focus of the family was on his illness and my mother's nervous disposition. I had simply become a wallflower, painfully shy, rarely speaking to anyone.

However, I felt guilty for having those feelings towards my brother and mother, feeling that I was in some way being very selfish, and I began telling myself that I was a bad person. I continued my visits to the Jehovah's Witnesses and wanted to hear more about their coming Kingdom that would solve all of my problems. They impressed upon me that my family would not be saved in the coming battle of Armageddon. Even though that message was disturbing to me, I felt safe, for I would no longer have to suffer in their presence. I was fifteen or sixteen at the time.

A year or two later, when my father had great financial difficulties, the family became homeless. Following a nervous breakdown, my mother had gone to live with a friend; my brother was once again in a psychiatric hospital; and my eldest brother, whom I adored and worshipped as my hero, was no longer living in the UK but in the Middle East. During that period, my father worked nights as a taxi driver and stayed with his sister. Despite my parents' reservations, I was allowed to go and live with a family of

Jehovah's Witnesses so that I could continue my schooling. But life with this family became as much a hell as living with my own family had been. The mother seemed bitter and resentful of her husband's activity in the church, and her children were cold and unfriendly towards me. I got up at five o'clock in the morning to deliver newspapers and generally worked after school until five or six in the evening, plus all day on Saturday. At the end of the week when I received my pay, a princely sum of thirteen pounds, I would give the mother ten pounds and keep three for myself. Yet she constantly complained that she was not being paid enough to look after me. There were also times when she would serve up meat, vegetables and potatoes for her children and beans on toast for me. All of this gave me the feeling that I was simply not wanted, not welcomed by anyone at all. This feeling was to become the cornerstone of my view of the world and of my beliefs concerning myself.

I also had problems at school during my time with this family. Not only was I bullied by a couple of the other boys; I would often receive detention for falling asleep in class. It was only later that I learnt that during a visit to the doctor at the age of sixteen I had been prescribed valium, and taking this was the whole reason for my falling asleep in class! During my six- or seven- month stay with this family, I was often left at home alone as their children went on outings with other teenagers from the Jehovah's Witness church; I was again being ostracized for asking too many questions and for being "self important". I did not see my mother at all during that period and my father visited sporadically. However, my spirits were lifted during one visit that my eldest brother and hero made whilst he was visiting London from his home in the Middle East.

I left school at seventeen with very few qualifications to my name. The valium, the bullying, and my life of misery and absolute loneliness had taken their toll. In addition, the family that I had been staying with impressed upon me that their "Kingdom" was coming soon so it was better for me to forego the temptations that abounded at universities and colleges. The lack of qualifications simply added to my sense of worthlessness and I developed quite a chip on my shoulder later in life for not having been to university or having some sort of degree. This meant that I had to excel at everything I did, for without the piece of paper that stated that I had some value, I felt of little value.

All in all, when I considered the actions of the family I stayed with and my own family, and the inaction of school teachers concerning the bullying, I felt that no one, not a single soul on the entire planet, had one shred of caring, concern or love for me – nor did God. The combination of physical, sexual, emotional and religious abuse left an indelible mark on that sensitive teenager. All of this led me to desperately seek approval from everyone and anyone, just to feel visible, seen. I longed for someone, anyone, just to notice that I was alive and that I had feelings.

I left the family I had been staying with and returned to my parents who were now living together again in a new home. Unfortunately for me, my very sick brother was there, as well. The violence started all over again. My parents, having dug themselves out of a financial hole, decided to go on holiday for ten days to Florida, leaving me and my brother alone in the house together for that period. Were they, too, insane? It was only a day or two after their departure that he beat me so severely that I remember crawling on my hands and knees towards the telephone and calling the police. He had been shouting and screaming that he wanted to kill me; luckily, the police turned up just in time. Rather than being rescued, though, I was told that they could not interfere with domestic violence and, as I was officially an adult at the delicate age of just eighteen, they left. Yet again, the feeling of being invisible, not important, not cared for sank in along with a gaping feeling of emptiness. At eighteen, not clearly understanding the laws of the land at the time, it seemed to me that not even the men in blue cared about what happened to me. I did not return to the house but simply walked away. I walked to the house of a man who was an elder in the Jehovah's Witness church. He and his wife offered me refuge. I had no clothes with me other than those I was wearing; as I was too afraid to return home, I wore the same clothes for almost a week until the date that I knew my parents would return. I went home and, as before, the matter was never discussed. I was not consoled but instead, from my viewpoint, was simply ignored.

When all of this happens on a constant basis, the belief that we are not loved transforms into the belief that somehow, in some way, we have become unlovable. I began to question what was wrong me. Surely, there had to be something wrong with me. Otherwise others would care what happened to me. As it appeared that they neither cared nor even noticed that I was alive and breathing, I came to the conclusion that it must be all my fault, that there was something so intrinsically wrong with me that this is what I deserved. I had heard a lot about God punishing us for our sins, so the natural conclusion for me to make was that I was being punished for being bad in some way — so of course it must be my fault. I concluded that it was my own fault for simply being gay, and that this was at the root of my suffering. My self- esteem plummeted and my sense of being unworthy of anything good increased.

I had become aware that I was gay at about the age of eight. I distinctly remember telling the little girl next door whom I played dolls with that I wanted to marry a man when I grew up. As these feelings were present long before the sexual abuse, I was satisfied that it was my nature and not learnt behaviour as a result of the abuse. Owing to my religious beliefs, I prayed every night that this curse of being gay would be lifted from me so that I would not either go to the Catholic hell or be destroyed during the Jehovah's Witness Armageddon. Not only had I received the message from my family that I was of no importance; religion had also told me that my very nature was at best wrong, and at worst evil and only worthy of damnation.

There were times when I convinced myself that having a sex change would be the solution to all of my problems. I knew that I could not change my feelings, so I turned my discomfort towards loathing my body, feeling convinced that, if only I had been born into a female body, none of my problems would exist. In the mind of a lonely and traumatized teenager, a sex change was the perfect solution. I could become a woman, marry a good Christian man and not burn in hell, for then I would no longer be a sinner. During this period my sense of loneliness grew deeper and deeper and I spent most of my free time outside of work riding around on my bicycle, for I was not good at making friends, and my conviction was that no one wanted me anyway.

One hot Saturday afternoon I stopped off at a pub in full spandex cycling shorts and had a Coca-Cola. Everyone was very friendly and I was offered several drinks by the men who were standing outside on the pavement. It was not until I rode off on my bike that I realized that I had just visited my first gay pub. I was delighted at how friendly everyone was and I thought that, if that was what gay meant, being very friendly, then it couldn't be all that bad. I was so naïve that it took me quite a while to figure out that a fit-looking young man in spandex would attract a lot of attention and that their friendliness had another meaning altogether.

A few weeks later, I met a man called Eddie and I had sex for the first time with a man of my choice. However, still being an active Jehovah's Witness, I was racked with guilt and I decided that I should confess to the elders of the church. What followed was harrowing, to say the least. They quoted me Bible passages regarding confession and insisted that I divulge my sin in every detail. Yes, they wanted to know *every* intimate detail; they asked me questions like, "Who was the girl and who was the boy?" and asked about oral sex and anal sex in all manner of detail. I felt totally humiliated and was commanded to attend the Kingdom Hall on that very Sunday. When I arrived at the hall and the meeting started, my confession was read out loud to the entire congregation and all young men were told not to speak to me until I was fully repented. As a result, the only two young men that I had been friendly with were lost to me as friends. I was alone again. The confession, followed by the public humiliation, coupled with my own experience of sexual abuse, only served to make me take on a lot of shame regarding my own sexuality. The shame was another belief that would influence many of my adult relationships and much of my sexual conduct as I got older.

A few weeks later, the ban on speaking to me was lifted, but it didn't change much; people simply never greeted me and I was no longer invited to any church functions. An elder in the church took me under his wing and began to counsel me on my sexuality. The sum total of his advice was that I should marry, and that is exactly what I did at the age of nineteen. The marriage was short-lived: about ten days – for obvious reasons.

I remained in the church, and this time I was on probation. I had to carry out even more "Christian" duties, such as selling *The Watchtower* magazine and knocking on doors as much as I could in order to show my repentance. However, I slipped once again when Jean-Paul entered my life – well, only for a weekend. He was sweet and kind. After we had had sex, I gave him my telephone number. His response was to laugh. He explained to me rather harshly that it was "just sex" and then asked me to leave. I was devastated, for in my mind he was now my boyfriend. I was desperate for any kind of affection. I again confessed to the elders and this time I was excommunicated. In one fell swoop I lost all of my friends. Even a dear friend of mine, John, refused to open his front door to me when I called by to visit. I lived life feeling that neither God nor my parents nor my friends loved me and that I was a condemned man with the sword of Damocles hanging over me. At that time I was renting a room just a mile or so from the office where I worked as a clerk, and I spent many a night on the phone to the Samaritans as I was seriously contemplating suicide. Life was simply not worth living, even at the age of nineteen.

In the years that followed I went from one bad relationship to the next, including a three-year relationship with an alcoholic who beat me on a regular basis. To this day, I have reduced hearing in my right ear owing to a severe beating I received. In hindsight, I believe I stayed with him because it was what I knew. Having left my teenage years feeling totally alone, unloved and unworthy, my belief system allowed me to accept just anyone as a partner, for I truly did not feel that I was worthy of anything better. The fact that I was unworthy, to my mind, had been demonstrated abundantly by my parents, my brother, the police, my school, the general practitioner that put me on valium, and, of course, the two churches I had been associated with. When things like this happen to us as young people and teenagers, it is very easy for us to form beliefs about the world that become a set pattern until such time as we come to the realization that we can change the beliefs, and therefore change our world.

In my very early twenties, the years were peppered with experimenting with drugs like marijuana, speed and LSD – anything to numb the pain I was in. During my time with the alcoholic, I began to gain weight; when I was not numbing my pain with alcohol or drugs, I was numbing it with food. I was rather successful in my career and earned a lot of money in the boom years of the eighties. I had become the archetypal yuppie. However, no matter how much money I earned, no matter how many expensive suits, shoes and gadgets I owned, nothing but food would numb the pain. As I began to gain weight, the self-loathing I had felt, not only as a result of my sexual abuse but also from the time I had wanted to have a sex change, returned full force. I could not bear to look into mirrors and avoided them at all costs. What the food and the weight gain had done was simply to place a spotlight on a feeling that was already present – the belief that I was ugly. The more I ate, the uglier I felt; the uglier I felt, the more I ate in an attempt to cover up the feeling. On the inside I felt valueless, unlovable, totally worthless. I simply confirmed those beliefs to myself by allowing others to treat me that way.

Directly after ending the relationship with my alcoholic boyfriend, I moved to Holland and met a wonderful gentle man with whom I lived for ten years. This relationship, too, became unhappy. I totally lost myself in trying to accommodate his culture as much as possible and pretty much became a Dutch housewife. He was very critical and a perfectionist so, naturally, I never measured up. Because I felt so worthless, it was easy for me to become whatever he wanted me to become, for who I was, was of no value anyway. Very often, after a day of housework, I would wait nervously at home for him to return. Predictably, he would find fault with something; it was what I had come to expect. As a gay man, I have noticed that many women are in the habit of accepting this, too, for the sake of having a man in their lives. It's the same programming, the same belief system: without a man at my side, I am a nobody.

In the first year of our relationship I discovered that this man was not faithful, and this was yet another devastating blow to my self-esteem. Instead of leaving, I remained, for I was truly convinced that I had nowhere to go. I was convinced that this was as good as it gets and was probably all the love I would ever have, so I decided to stay. This, of course gave him permission to do what he wished to do, for I was going to stay anyway. Instead of leaving, I began to eat again in order to numb my pain, and then my fear of the dreaded mirror increased. It was also during this period of my life that I first came across alternative therapy, metaphysical concepts, and eventually Family Constellation work, and my life began to change little by little, until, at last, I ended the relationship upon discovering yet another of his "indiscretions". I began to realize that I had agreed to it all, that I could have walked out two weeks into the relationship, the very first time he had an "indiscretion".

I began to see that, although I had had no control of the abuse experienced during childhood, I did have control of the abuse I was experiencing in my adult life. Furthermore, I had *allowed* it all to happen. There was no one to blame except myself, but I had already done enough self-blaming. The first time the alcoholic beat me and I did nothing, I was simply telling him, "I'm worthless, go ahead", and it was that same message I gave to the man who continued to play the field. At the end of the day, it all came down to me. I was the only person that could change any of this. I learnt that I had a choice as to whether I wanted to be a victim, or draw the line and say, in effect, "this far and no further". However, in order to have the courage to do this, I had to change my core beliefs about myself, despite all the evidence that appeared to confirm what I was feeling and believing.

To sum up, I spent my childhood years, right through my twenties and thirties and into my early forties, feeling worthless, loathing my body, and feeling weighed down by the shameful secrets I held. I placed all of my self-worth into just having a man in my life, and therefore I accepted relationships that were not supportive – just so that I would not feel the nagging, deep loneliness within me. There had been drugs, violence, promiscuity, extravagance, many thoughts of suicide – all because I had believed the direct and indirect messages I had received from churches, my parents and other authorities. I spent those years so far from the presence of my own soul, that I might as well have lived in an abyss of total darkness, which is what my life felt like most of the time.

One of the most difficult challenges I had to deal with was my loathing and hatred for my brother. Often as a teenager and in my early twenties I would fantasize about going to his funeral and spitting on his coffin. Living with this level of hatred towards another human being was a weight in itself, and one that I would have to painfully deal with. Today I have a totally different perspective on our relationship and he now has a place in my heart, but it took much work to get to this place with him.

Like many women, I as a gay man learned to loathe my body, for it did not conform to media images of what was beautiful. Within the gay community I was subject to much nastiness owing to how I looked, and it often struck me as odd that we had a gay rights movement when so many gay men were prepared to treat other gay men with total disdain, simply based on looks. I so longed to look like the men that were depicted in the gay media and in pornography. I so longed to be thought of as sexy and handsome instead of loathsome and ugly, which was the way I felt. My belief was that if I looked like the men in the pictures, then surely I would find someone to love me. What I did not realize at the time was that if they loved me for my body alone, that was not love at all and I would simply end up back where I started.

As gay men have been taught such self-loathing by parents, by religious teachings and by society in general, for many, the only thing they possess that could be considered beautiful is their body. This is one of the illnesses of the gay community and I bought into it by believing that I was of no value to the gay community, either, for the only thing that could be beautiful about me was not in the least bit beautiful, but fat and grotesque. I realized that not only was there racism in the world, homophobia and sexism; "fat-ism" also existed. If you were fat, you were less than the others, which is ironic, considering I was far "more" than most – at least when it came to my waistline.

What is important to state here is that, although I am introducing these subjects from the perspective of being a gay man, the belief systems and the self-doubt we take on as a result are universal. Each and every one of us, male or female, straight or gay, succumbs to images and beliefs about what is good, beautiful and worthy. Through the years, owing to poor body image and a feeling of being totally contemptible, I allowed myself not only to get involved in relationships with men that were totally unsuitable for me, but also to engage in sexual activities that were the opposite of what I truly wanted. My thinking was, if I do this or that to please him, then he will love me in return. You know, it never worked. Whenever we compromise our dignity for the sake of pleasing another in the vain attempt of gaining their love and affection, we end up empty-handed. Love does not work that way. It never has, and it never will.

What happened was that my sense of shame simply grew deeper, along with my self-loathing. Even as I began my career as a teacher, writer and motivational speaker, the one thing that I never wanted my clients or audience to know about me was my abyss of shameful secrets – the way I felt about my body. I was smart, witty, highly intuitive and insightful, but I had also built up a level of defences around me – arrogance being the primary one – for it did not matter how much praise I received, how many accolades were bestowed upon me, or how successful I was: I felt like a total fraud because of my shameful secrets. I convinced myself that if only I could be better at what I did, appear better to the world, then the feeling would go away. I really had missed the point. It was changing the inside that would change the outside.

Shameful Secrets

Each of us carries shameful secrets and we do our utmost to disguise and hide them. The most important thing to know about shameful secrets is that it is *the shame itself* that is the greater secret, greater than the events that led to it. The longer we hold onto our shameful secrets, the larger and more powerful they become, until they begin to control many aspects of our life. Many of today's shameful secrets are concerning the body, self-image, and the shame we took on as children. We can be high-flying executives, famous authors, successful business people, television presenters or the perfect husband, father, wife or mother, and still be holding onto shameful secrets in the furthest reaches of our minds. Shameful secrets can come from feelings of not being worthy, not being loved or simply not being good enough. Perhaps we were sexually abused, shamed in public by a parent, sibling or a school teacher, or perhaps we grew up in a family where we felt totally unloved.

If you are reading this book, then you have more than likely been through some therapy or have done some inner work in order to resolve one or more issues that you may have. However, in all of my experience of working both on myself and with others, very little is gained until we begin to really dig deep and root out the shameful secrets we hold about ourselves. What I have learnt is that, when we hold onto and protect our shameful secrets, this is what we project out into the world and it becomes more and more a part of our experience and reality. In other words, as we try in vain to hide our shame, the more our shame is exposed, through the events that we create and attract into our lives.

Let me give an example. In the mid-nineties, the thing I hated most was going shopping for clothing. I always felt awkward, especially when I had to leave a shop after discovering that they had nothing in my size. One Saturday afternoon I went with my then-boyfriend to buy a new pair of jeans. I entered the store and started looking for trousers. A young male shop assistant, who was clearly gay, came up to me and asked if I needed any help. I told him that I needed some new trousers, to which he replied, "We have nothing for you, you are simply too fat for this store". I literally dropped the clothes I did have in my possession and walked as quickly as possible outside, tears rolling down my face, to my boyfriend who was standing on the pavement having a cigarette. I told him what was wrong and his was response was to say, "Well, he didn't lie, you are too fat!" I felt shamed and betrayed all over again. My constant fear of being shamed in this way simply led to much more of it happening, and I agreed to more shame by remaining in a relationship with a man who shamed me on a constant basis. I had to come to terms with the fact that I had agreed to the shame, and the more I said yes to it, the more it happened. The events of my childhood meant that I grew accustomed to being shamed and accepted it as part of my reality. What I have learnt is that *whatever* we accept as being true for ourselves will happen over and over and over again, until we change our inner picture. Not only do we attract the circumstances into our lives through the Law of Attraction, but we also give others permission by default to treat us in shameful ways. The first time we don't say "no" to something that another does, we're actually telling them that it is okay for them to do that.

As I learnt and understood more, I realized that I could not have so much shame and at the same time come from a family that had no shame. As I entered Family Constellation and trans-generational healing work, it became clear to me that not only were my parents deeply shamed, but that it had been going on for generations. Somehow, I had to find the courage to be happier than my mother and my brother, and give myself permission to become that.

This book is about how we take on belief systems from our families and live them out as if they are our own, attracting the events and people in our lives that deepen the experience of shame, guilt and a host of other feelings. I have also provided tools and exercises that you can use in order to start or continue with the process of liberation from shame, self-doubt, depression and low self-esteem, and start moving in the direction of consciously creating your own reality.

As I've used these methods myself, I have discovered the gentleness in my heart and my love for other people. I have allowed myself to be helped and assisted by others, instead of hiding my "weaknesses" with shame. I have also discovered much beauty and courage within the spirit of humanity and likewise have allowed myself to see myself as having much beauty and courage. The path of healing is the road less traveled as we are often very afraid of our pain; however, pretending that it is not there, or hiding it, simply makes things worse. On the other hand, living out our pain with drama and with self-pity is also not the solution. The solution is to face it head on, look at the hidden gifts and acknowledge them, and then make choices concerning what we really want to believe about ourselves. As we make these choices, what manifests in our lives begins to change.

Today, I am in a very different place. I still struggle with my weight, and that struggle may stay with me for the rest of my life – or it may not. I haven't found solutions to all of my problems yet, but I've found many. I am a work in progress. Today, I truly love my work and feel worthy of it, and I no longer feel the need to hide anything from anyone. I also no longer feel the need to date men that are totally unsuitable for me. I no longer *need* his love, or rather, the illusion of what I thought love was. Love is kind, gentle, supportive and does not criticize or shame others. Accepting less than this is no longer acceptable.

How far are you willing to go in order to ensure that you are living a life that is truly worth living? My journey has taken me from feeling void of any sense of soul, to embarking on a journey in which there has been a gradual unfolding of the presence of my own soul within me.

What is very important to say here is that we must understand the difference between the facts of what happened and our stories around what happened. A fact is an event that actually occurred; a story is our interpretation of the motivations of others involved in the event. For example, I have made it clear that my feeling and conclusion was that I was not loved or cared for. That is not a fact, for I cannot know the inner feelings of another. What we decide are the actions of love may not be what constitutes love for another; therefore when we interpret the feelings and motivations of others according to their actions, or inactions as the case may be, we are creating a story. Stories become prisons, as is abundantly evident in what I have shared with you in this introduction. My belief systems were built upon the conclusions I made according to the evidence as I experienced it. Our job is to disentangle ourselves from our stories and re-define the beliefs that we have chosen for ourselves. It is my solid belief that there are very few deliberately malicious people on the planet who seek to hurt others with intent; we simply do what we know how to do, until we know differently.

With love,
John L. Payne

INTRODUCTION

EXPRESSION OF THE SOUL

Often, when we think of the term "soul", we consider it to be that part of us that will live on after the demise of our physical body. We often give little thought to the presence of our soul as we live day to day. The scope of this book is not to discuss the eternal validity of the soul, the afterlife or reincarnation, except in brief. Although I personally subscribe to those beliefs, my main purpose here is to relate to you how the presence of the soul in our day-to-day lives has been communicated to me through working with many individuals over several years.

Through my work, I have witnessed that the prevailing principle of the soul is expressed through *inclusiveness* and that the primary communication of the soul is through *simplicity* and *distilled truth*.

As the soul reveals itself, it becomes apparent that it is not a part of us that we will only discover as our consciousness re-focuses itself into a nonphysical reality. Rather, through our conscious practice, choices, thoughts and words, we can experience the essence of our true selves in our day-to-day lives and allow our soul to be our guide and companion. Many believe that this can only be achieved through rigorous training in one or another meditation technique, or that they are so far removed from that mystical part of themselves that knowing their soul is far beyond their reach. However, I have observed that applying the simple principles of *inclusiveness* and *distilled truth* in our lives can make the presence of our soul very real as we clear out the clutter in our relationships, thoughts and feelings. The presence of the soul can be experienced when we allow the qualities of inclusiveness, allowing and truth to guide our lives.

The purpose of this book is to communicate how you can incorporate the principles and essence of a soul-driven life simply by reading this book and putting into practice some of the principles I will share with you.

Universal Inclusiveness

The soul is inclusive of all things, as has become abundantly evident to me through the practice of Family Constellation work. No one and no thing is ever excluded, neither victims nor perpetrators, well wishers nor those with mal-intent, neither the dead nor the living, the rich or the poor, the well or the unwell; everyone and everything is equal in the realm of the soul. For some, this is a difficult concept to grasp, as we have been raised in a culture that has been dominated by punitive religions for so long and we exist within a culture that insists on defining that which is good and allowed and that which is bad and forbidden. However, what we have witnessed is that *exclusion* has been at the root of much human suffering and pain. It was not so long ago when young unwed mothers were secreted away and much shame was put upon them and their children denied their rightful place in the world with the use of terms like "illegitimate". Today, we see the rise of Neo-Nazism in some parts of German society as a result of the exclusion of the Nazis and their place in German history and society. The underlying principle of the soul dictates that that which is excluded, will be included or represented. This can also be expressed in the popular saying: that which you resist, persists.

History has taught us that the exclusion of anything has far-reaching effects. There was a time when Africans and Australian aboriginals were defined as cattle or livestock, denied the presence or acknowledgement of their own soul; similarly with the Jews and, in times gone by, parallel thinking between Catholics and Protestants and many other groups. On the grander scale of human events, you may be wondering, how do we include the unthinkable and despicable? How do we give a place in our hearts to the many perpetrators in our world? How do we find a place in our hearts for the Nazis, the architects of apartheid, the perpetrators of genocide in Bosnia or Rwanda, and the likes of Stalin, to name but a few?

The question that we really need to ask is this: Do we deny those groups and individuals a soul? Or do we look with compassion at the devastating effect that their actions have had on their own soul and on their descendants? When we exclude perpetrators through deciding that they have no soul, or no longer have the right to be considered human, our posturing becomes akin to that of the slave traders of old who decided wholesale that their "merchandise" possessed no soul; in other words, we take on and express perpetrator energy. At the root of all world disputes is the self-proclaimed "good" or "right" taking a stance against the "bad" or "wrong". Many will argue that it is clear that the Nazis were bad, and, certainly, there is overwhelming evidence to support that belief. However, when we the "good" determine who is "bad", we become just like them. We often justify righteous indignation – which only serves the purpose of adding more polarization to the world instead of inclusiveness. Through observation, I have frequently found that we tend to imitate those whom we least respect.

In observing the devastating effects upon the souls and families of perpetrators, which can have far reaching consequences for many generations, I have asked myself, for whom do we mourn? Do we only mourn for the Jews, the Poles, the Gypsies, the gay men and women and the countless others that suffered the fate of the Nazi concentration camps, or do we also mourn for the Nazis and their families? Just as I have seen that the children and grandchildren of Holocaust survivors can have a deep sense of having lost their soul, so I have found it also true of the children and grandchildren of those involved in the Nazi war machine. Our society encourages the mourning of victims, for it is "the right thing to do", and yet it is clear that there is a price to be paid when we forget the souls of the perpetrators. Through observation and practice it has become abundantly clear to me that in order to achieve balance in the world we also need to mourn the perpetrators.

It behooves us to step back and imagine for a moment the consequences of exclusionary actions, and the damage that they do to the human soul. The effects are devastating and far- reaching.

During one workshop, I had the privilege of working with a young woman whose life had been marred by years of depression and deep-seated feelings of unworthiness. As I investigated her family history, she revealed that her grandfather, although a regular German army foot soldier, had been placed on duty on a watchtower in Auschwitz. As our work together took form, it was apparent that her grandfather had the feeling of having lost his own soul through what he had observed and through the orders he had been obliged to carry out. This enduring and devastating feeling had passed to her from her grandfather via her mother. She reported that her great difficulty was that she felt that she had no permission to either love or acknowledge her grandfather, as the world at large had decided that individuals such as her grandfather could no longer be considered human, and that she felt guilty simply for being his granddaughter.

Whilst most of us can give a place in our hearts to this young woman, as she is clearly seen to be "innocent", our challenge almost always comes in giving a place to her grandfather, the "guilty" one. What I have observed through trans-generational healing work is that the feeling carried by the granddaughter is indeed the feeling that her grandfather had as a result of his experience. When we step back and look at such cases with the eyes of truth, it becomes clear that perpetrators, whether remorseful or not, live with the devastating effects of their actions. They have lost the awareness of their own soul and their sense of humanity. For this we must mourn, for it is truly a deeply tragic matter. When we mourn for the perpetrators, not only does it assist us to find our own soul and sense of humanity; it also gives permission to their descendants to count themselves once more as humans with a soul.

When we consider the Bible's words, "visiting the sins of the fathers upon the children, unto the third and the fourth generation", it becomes apparent that this knowledge of trans-generational transference of guilt, shame and remorse is not new. Mourning the perpetrators goes well beyond pity, for most of us can find pity within us for such individuals and groups. Pity, however, can often lack equality, given our tendency to look down upon such individuals. What is required is that we fully embrace the scale of the self-inflicted damage and all the resulting consequences. When we are in a place of being able to mourn the Jews and the Nazis equally, we can bring peace to ourselves as individuals and eventually to the world. Exclusion begets exclusion which in turn begets yet more inhumane action as victims become perpetrators and their victims do likewise. When the cycle of exclusion ceases, so, too, will the cycle of victims and perpetrators.

Whether our exclusion is of Nazis, Islamic terrorists, pedophiles, the architects of apartheid, murderers, or a specific ethnic group, the solution and the effects remain the same. The loss that has occurred is borne not only by the victims.

Personal Inclusiveness

Whilst it may be relatively easy for us to embrace *universal inclusiveness* as expressed in the previous section, most of us are more challenged when it comes to the area of *personal inclusiveness*. I define personal inclusiveness as allowing and embracing individuals in our lives who have hitherto been excluded. Let me give you an example. I worked with a woman who reported having problems with her young teenage children. She shared that they were disruptive, defiant and almost always angry with her. As her story unfolded, she told me that her husband had had an affair with a colleague at work and had left her to live with the other woman. Surprisingly, rather than the children being angry with their father out of loyalty to their mother (which often happens), it transpired that the children were really angry with her. Let me explain. Whilst we can understand that my client would not be the best of friends with her former husband, it became apparent that she had excluded her ex-husband from the role of being a father to the children, demanding an unspoken loyalty from her children with the expectation that they, too, would exclude him. The source of the children's anger was feeling that they were being denied a father. Her ex-husband's position as the children's father is a given, not something that can ever be undone, and when we attempt to exclude that which is, it always has consequences, some of which my client was living with. Many would argue that to include the ex-husband as the father (an undeniable fact) is to sanction or condone his behaviour. However, the actions of individuals do not define their rightful place. No matter the action, the father remains the father. When we exclude such fathers, we in effect punish the children for something they have no control over – nor indeed is it any of their business. I have often observed that when one in a couple seeks to punish the other through exclusion, they themselves will be punished by their children, as was the case with my client.

In families there are often those that have been excluded or forced into the role of "black sheep". I have observed that when we exclude anyone, we exclude a part of ourselves. One client reported that she had great difficulty with her relationship with her sister, as her sister made a living as an exotic dancer in a strip club. As we worked on this topic, it was clear that my client had difficulties with her own sexuality and indeed excluded many of her own feelings and natural impulses. What was interesting was that her children loved their aunt and were very fond of her, and became very excited whenever she visited. Her children, in their innocence and natural ability to include with love, had the impulse to abundantly display their inclusion of their aunt to counterbalance their mother's exclusion.

When we include, we feel more complete and whole. Exclusion always leaves a hole.

Throughout life we are challenged to include many individuals and behaviours that we would otherwise feel pressured or expected to exclude, such as a drug-taking sibling, an alcoholic, a thief, a prostitute, a father or mother who had affairs, an ex-partner or spouse, and many more. We may feel that we are inclusive of such individuals or behaviours when we state that we are trying to help such individuals overcome their alcoholism or whatever their particular habit or lifestyle choice has been. However, when we look closely and realize that our helping may not be fully at the request of the other, we have simply uncovered another layer of disallowing, or exclusion.

Inclusiveness is really about non-judgement. However, many of us fail in this area, especially when we say things like, "I don't judge it, I simply don't like it", in which case we are simply tolerating it.

When we tolerate we still have negative emotion around the subject and, when negative emotion exists, there is no freedom. The only thing that we need to like or not like is that which is directly within our own experience – meaning, if being an alcoholic does not align with our own life preferences, then it is not for us. However, the business of others is simply that, someone else's business. They are capable of making choices for themselves. The less we worry about other people's choices and keep out of their business, the more fruitful and joyous our own lives can be. As we do this, then our contribution to the planet is one of a joyful life. As soon as we exclude anything, any behaviour, any person, race, creed, event or culture, we go into resistance and our life does not flow as we want it to, for our creative energies are tied up in resistance instead of being focused on creating the harmony that we desire.

Simplicity and Distilled Truth

Another important principle behind experiencing the presence of the soul is *simplicity*. Many of us get very involved in our stories of how we believe things to be, how we believe others to be, and how we believe the world to be. Stories have a way of getting bigger and bigger and, the more we talk about them, the more dominant they become, leaving us often entrapped and imprisoned by them. Our stories become our scripts; they colour our vision and perception, determine our choices, burden us with fear, resentment, and perhaps bitterness and anger. However, when we look more closely at out stories, they often have very little substance and truth. When we tell our story often enough, we lose track of what is really true and what is simply perception, very often making our own personal perceptions of a moment in time into an undeniable and irrefutable truth. This self-created truth then begins to define us and the world that we live in, but for the most part it only serves to limit us – though we often don't realize that our stories are doing just that, limiting us.

Our thoughts are magnetic to other similar thoughts, meaning that when we have an idea or a thought of something, we naturally acquiesce to our own inner reference point and gather other thoughts and ideas that are similar to it. If you have ever played the imaginary game of winning the lottery, you will understand that things just get better and better and bigger and bigger when you consider what you will do with your prize. You start off by saying that you will pay off all your debts, then you'll buy a new car, and the more excited you get, you add a new house, no, a ten-bedroom mansion, then a speedboat and, on top of it all, you will travel the world. So it is with our negative stories. If your story is, "My mother was cold and didn't show affection", the next addition to the story is, "My mother didn't love me", which then turns into, "I was not good enough to be loved", then, "No one loves me", and on to "The world is an unlovable place", or "I always choose partners who do not love me". At this stage, our story has become not only our point of perception and understanding of the world, and therefore the filter through which we interpret all of our experiences and interactions with others, but also our script and our point of attraction in terms of experience. A life script, just like the script in a play or a movie, determines the role of the main character (you) and how the other characters will interact with you. When our story becomes our script, and we all have many of these scripts, we become convinced that our perceptions are absolute reality when, in fact, most if not all of our original stories are simply stories, not provable with certainty or fact.

At times, we can have so much invested in our life scripts and stories that healing can itself become sabotaged as we fall into the dead-end trap of the "yes, but" syndrome. The "yes, but" trap is something that we often use to resist change or when we get stuck in the need for others (or the world) to change in order for us to be happy.

Through my work with many individuals over several years, I have witnessed that healing is created by the embracing of simple truths that do not carry the weight of stories or our scripts. For example, individuals that are divorced from their spouses often have a lot invested in the story of the relationship and the marriage and the reasons why the divorce happened, which gives justification or reason to their anger. However, the story more often than not is devoid of the facts of the relationship. The simple truth is the following: "There was once great love between us, and it is a great pity that it has been lost". This is an example of *distilled truth;* when it can be acknowledged, then the healing process can begin.

The presence of the soul is also evident with simplicity. We often overlook the simplicity of love when we have our attention focused on the expectation that things will be greater than they actually are, or our desires are focused on wanting far more than most people are able to offer us. When we overlook simple pleasures and the simplicity and ordinariness of love in human relationships, our attention turns to lack and our scripts are created. Love is not a secret, it is all around us, and it is ordinary. It is your partner or best friend bringing you chicken soup when you are sick, it is someone holding up an umbrella for you when it rains, it is a friend calling to ask you how you are doing or complimenting your new shoes. Simple and uncomplicated love is around us at all times. It is only our stories and the ones we've made into life scripts that stop us from seeing it.

Love flows when we communicate in simple ways. When we are angry with someone, love is able to flow when we say, "I felt disappointed when you didn't show up for my birthday party'", rather than creating a whole story around the event that simply gets bigger and bigger until the one that didn't show up is transformed in your thinking to be like the mother you so despised, and the friend ends up paying the price for yet another of our stories that has become a life script. Simple communication regarding what displeases us goes hand in hand with simple appreciation. The clearer and simpler we can be, the more love can flow. As we become clearer and more succinct in our communication with others, the more others will respond to us in like manner. We will no longer have to listen to their long stories that explain just why they didn't show up for our birthday party; they will simply say, "I'm sorry" and mean it, offering you an uncomplicated truth.

There is great evidence around us that simple love is alive and well. All we need do is acknowledge it. Simply.

Through the pages of this book, we will take a journey to uncover hidden loyalties and learn how to embrace simple appreciation and simple abundance. The more uncomplicated we make the story of our lives, the more we can begin to witness the magic of life itself and begin to live a magical life.

Furthermore, I will take you on a journey where you will begin to see, understand and *feel* how your beliefs about life create your direct experience of it – indeed, create your reality. You will begin to understand how beliefs are transferred trans-generationally and how it is that so many generations of your family may have created the same circumstances in their lives, not by pure co-incidence, but owing to powerful beliefs that are created through trauma and the difficult life experiences of previous generations. This book holds many keys to unlocking those things that bind you to living an unfulfilled or ordinary life, so that you may be freed to experience the magic of life.

> *If you can't explain it simply,*
> *you don't understand it well enough.*
>
> Albert Einstein

Chapter One

THE WORLD IS WHAT IT IS

When I was a young child living in Singapore I became acutely aware of the "haves" and the "have-nots". I often wondered why I was fortunate enough to have a nice home whilst others were much less fortunate and seemed to have much less than I did. The question "why?" stayed with me throughout my childhood, my teenage years and well into my twenties and thirties. Now, although my mind is often boggled by the vastness of the night sky over Africa, the question of why has less and less significance in my life. Not all of my questions have been answered, but I've come to the conclusion that the world is what it is. Reaching this conclusion and submitting to the fact that many things will remain a mystery, I have felt great liberation. I no longer buy into the idea that I have a special mission in life, that the world needs saving, or that large groups or individuals need rescuing in some way. A dear friend of mine, Hilda, has impressed this upon me with frequent use of this reminder: "Unless you hear the words 'please help me', then mind your own business".

Over the past sixteen years, I could perhaps say that I've been on a spiritual quest. I say "perhaps", as my perspective on what a spiritual quest is has shifted enormously over the past eight or nine years of working with trans-generational healing and Family Constellation work. My spiritual quest has shifted from the search for "God" or "enlightenment" to realizing that all along I was really wanting to understand the world and my place in it. Paradoxically, it is that very shift from the external "God" to myself that has given me a greater understanding of the nature of our universe, life and the all-pervasive force and intelligence that is around us – we could call it "God", if we wish, or simply "Life".

Whilst on my spiritual quest I was introduced to many concepts, one of which was that of reincarnation. It made instant sense to me for I could not get to grips with the notion that we have only one shot at having a happy and fulfilled life or at "getting it right". As I explored the concept of reincarnation, I noticed that many of the belief systems around reincarnation were very similar to some of the punitive teachings of western religions – in other words, if you get it wrong, the universe, or "God", will punish you. Instead of hellfire, purgatory and damnation, we now had karma and the fear of a miserable time in the next incarnation if we in some way offended "God" in this incarnation. It struck me that much Eastern thought was just the same as Western thought, but wearing a different frock! On the surface, very different, but underneath, very similar – get it wrong and you'll either go to hell or live in a hell of your own making next time around. It took me several years to get out of the belief that if in some way I could be "more spiritual", then I would be assured a better place in the next life. I began to realize that by striving to be "more spiritual" I was really missing the point – actually, missing the world and the ordinariness of love. Very often, when we see ourselves as being spiritual, we see ourselves as being in some way special, perhaps a cut above the rest of the world. It dawned on me that that was not love at all, but arrogance pretending to be spiritual – in other words, piety. I cringed at that thought! How could I be so far off the mark? Well, simply put, we have learnt that we need to be, become or do a certain thing in order to be considered worthy, and I, like most of us on the planet, had bought into this idea.

My shift in perception and understanding came one afternoon when I was in deep meditation. I had gone into meditation with burning questions regarding the nature of things, why some countries were different than others, why terrible things happened in some places and to some people and not in other places or to other people, and why some people and governments seemed so "unenlightened". I asked about war, famine, disease, despotic governments, the Holocaust, etc. What I received as an answer made complete sense to me and still makes sense to me today. I was shown in a movie-like set of images how a soul arrives on planet earth as a baby soul, then gains experience through many lifetimes and matures to become an adolescent, a young, a mature and finally an old soul. What I realized was that just as my own focus in life has shifted from one life stage to the next, so it was for us as souls. We shift from surviving in a strange world, learning all the rules, to all the drama of our teenage years, to our drive and wanting to get ahead in our twenties, and then we begin to give up the need for power over others and the drama as we get older, having learnt many of life's lessons. Some months later, on a visit to South Africa, I met Hilda who was to become a dear friend. When I shared with her my insight about "soul ages", she handed me a book called *The Michael Handbook.* "It's all in here!" she exclaimed. I was delighted because not only had someone else had the same insight, but they had written a detailed handbook to understanding a particular view of human (soul) development and evolution.

As the years have passed, and with my in-depth experience of healing through trans-generational and Family Constellation work, I have begun to see that there are indeed greater forces at work in world events and how they affect the destinies of us all. When I refer to "greater forces", I do not refer to "the gods", but rather to the inner forces and momentum of humankind that create events that change the course of history and our future. Somehow, we all get swept along with them, just as our ancestors were, and the result is the life we are living today. This is what I call fate. Fate is not a prescription that is decided by the gods. Rather, each of us enters this world in a particular time or space that has a history and a precedence created by the generations that came before. What I've begun to see clearly is that the life we are living today and the circumstances in which we live are the result of the thoughts, ideas, wishes, dreams, experiences, feelings and actions of our ancestors; this is what I call fate. There is great misunderstanding about the word fate, as if it were a path that is set in stone and that pre-determines our entire lives. True, fate does determine our arrival in the world, for just as we cannot make the sun rise in the west and set in the east, we cannot change the parents we were born to or our ancestral heritage; these things are a given. The only thing we can change is how we feel about it all.

Fate is much greater than the individual, for it has the power to determine the course of nations, families and individuals – and history. When we become polarized in our view of world events and decide what is "right" and what is "wrong", we deny the very thing that has led to our being here and now, with the life that we have, in the form we have taken. For example, if you are an Irish-American, would your ancestors have arrived in America had it not been for the potato famine? If you are an Australian whose family has lived in Australia for many generations, what would have been your fate had Australia not been a penal colony and your great-great grandfather not been sent there for stealing a loaf of bread in England? You would not be an Australian and, perhaps, not in existence at all. The same is true for all of us. Without the winding river of history and its events, be those events World War II, the Holocaust, the pogroms, mass migration owing to oppression and poverty, African slavery, Spanish flu, or the Great Depression, to name but a few, the life that we have today would be very different. In fact, many of us would not have the opportunity to live life in the form we now have if the destinies of our ancestors had not been affected by such world events. With this concept in mind, how can we then say that anything that has happened in the past is "wrong"? We can't, for it is as it is.

When we challenge the fate that has led to what is, we challenge life itself and we deny who we are, to whom we were born and perhaps where we were born. The great forces of history and the desires, wishes, ideas and thoughts of our ancestors have literally created the life we have today. In other words, fate is life itself. It gives and it takes away. When we think of our personal lives, we often become aware of the twists of fate as we consider, for example, "Had I not met Bob, I would never have met Mary, and Mary would never have introduced me to Peter who later became the love of my life". If later we say, "I really don't like Bob and wish I had never met him", we then negate the gift that Bob gave us by proxy through Mary in the form of our great love Peter. And so it is for history and all the events that have happened down through time, even the ugliest of events. As part of my work, a great inner and deeply spiritual movement is to be able to bow with deep respect to history – be that African slavery, the Holocaust, the pogroms, the Irish potato famine, World War II, the persecution of the Huguenots, or the Roman Empire –, to our ancestors, and to whatever it is that shaped our destiny as the descendant of one or many persons whose life course was changed by such events.

When we look at the world, we see that we can do little or nothing about that much of what happens in the world. The pertinent question is, would we want to, or even, should we? Just as the events of history have acted like the butterfly effect* on our own lives, we have no idea of the forces behind current events that will shape the destinies of our descendants in generations to come. This does not mean to suggest that if we hear our neighbour crying out for help we should sit idly by and say, "It is her fate". On the contrary, we are moved by human compassion to step in and answer that call for help. We may also be motivated to donate money to an orphanage or to a school in need, but if at the same time we look at a child that has suffered and say to ourselves, "he deserved a better father", we stand in opposition to the forces of fate that are greater than ourselves whilst denying the truth of the child's life and ancestry. Fate must be respected. It is a force so much bigger than the individual, that to challenge it is to challenge the forces that govern all of human and other life on the planet.

If we were to travel back in time to the inception of our world, we would witness violent and cataclysmic events such as matter being spewed with great force from the body of our sun – not an event that life on our planet could survive today, yet it led to the very formation of our planet as we know it today. An erupting volcano in your back yard would not be seen as a good thing today, yet eruptions millions of years ago created beginnings of the atmosphere that we breathe today. So are exploding suns or volcanoes bad things? It all depends where in the time line of history and fate you are standing, and on your perspective in that moment in time. Could we imagine life on this planet had the dinosaurs not become extinct? Hardly! However, whilst it is easy for us to accept the blessing that the demise of the dinosaur has brought to humanity, difficulty often arises when we try to look at human-led events. We are shocked at the cruelty of some

---

* The phrase, "butterfly effect", refers to the idea that even a butterfly's fragile wings create tiny changes in the atmosphere that, through a chain of subsequent events, might ultimately cause – or prevent – a tornado, for example.

governments and the individuals within them, or we decry the abuse of children, or senseless crime and violence. This difficulty arises out of our expectation of how others should and could behave in comparison to how they are actually behaving. When we set ourselves apart as judge and jury when witnessing or hearing about such human behaviour, we ignore their fate. In other words, we cannot know the events down through the passages of time and their ancestors that have led to them becoming the perpetrators they are today. We truly cannot know anyone until we have walked a mile in their shoes. Surely they are responsible for their actions, but the real question is, given that we cannot fully know them, is their fate any of our business?

None of this precludes that when I witnessed through my television the genocide in Rwanda and in Bosnia, or the events of 9/11 as they unfolded, I was moved to tears of grief. However, I can choose to look at such events exactly as they are, events that cannot be changed, events that were spawned many years ago in a cascade that delivered the result that I am now a witness to. I could place all of my attention on thoughts and feelings that say, "It should never have happened" or perhaps get riled up in nationalism and thoughts of revenge, thereby adding to the sum of violent energy in the world; or, I can understand that just as I have my own fate, which is largely a mystery, so does everyone else on the planet.

The world is what it is and our contribution to the world and all life in it can be resistance to it if we so choose; or, we can contribute to the world through accepting fate and choosing to do something with the life that we have been given. We do not have a special God-given mission; we are not here to save the world, but rather to save ourselves from our negative viewpoints of the world and the events in it. We do not serve the poor by shunning wealth, we do not serve the sick by rejecting health, we do not serve the oppressed by limiting our own freedoms. We serve the world through choosing to live a joyous life despite all that is going on around us and in the lives of the people we know. Living a joyous life is the greatest contribution we can make to the world and it is the greatest way in which we can honour the life handed to us by our parents, ancestors and fate.

To date, as a species, we have not found a way to make great changes to our political, religious, social, philosophical and environmental habits and belief systems without creating sweeping change that causes suffering of many. In time, I believe that we will find a way. How long that will take, I have no real clue, but probably it won't be in my lifetime. Perhaps the next, or the one after that? In the future there will be challenges to be faced concerning the earth's precious resources, especially fresh clean water and our forests. Will nations go to war over water resources? Perhaps. Or will such shortages encourage nations to join hands, put aside their differences and learn from the suffering of the past?

At the end of our lives as we await the given fate of death, will we be worried if we were angry enough at 9/11, or incensed enough at the events in Rwanda, or worried if we had done enough for the poor? It is not likely. When we approach the closing of one door and the opening of another as our ancestors await us, our main question will be, Whom did I love, and did I love them well enough? This question puts the world and everything in it into perspective. We can choose to have that perspective now. Our contribution to the world can be to tell those we love that we love them, to say sorry to those that we need to say sorry to, to forgive those that we hold a grudge against, and to say thank you to all who have helped us in small ways and big ways. We can contribute worry and rage if we wish, but it won't make the world a better place. The world is what it is; we can only change ourselves and how we feel about it.

> *Everyone thinks of changing the world,*
> *but no one thinks of changing himself.*
>
> Leo Tolstoy

In the grand scheme of things, humanity is young; we've been here for fleeting moment of cosmic time and a mere minute or two in geological time. In the centuries that have gone by, we have seen empires rise and fall, cultures develop and fade away, religions rise up in the popular consciousness and disappear as quickly as they appeared. However, in many parts of the world today, consciousness is shifting, shifting away from the notion that if someone is not like ourselves, then they are either a threat or an enemy. The evolution of consciousness, whilst being a slow process over many generations, is gaining momentum. We need only to ask our grandmothers or mothers what their life and their expectations were as they grew up.

When we as seekers of alternative ways of thinking, being and doing sit back and judge the world for its "unenlightened" ways, we become just like those "others". The world is what it is. It has been around for some time and will continue to be around for some more time. However, even the planet, our sun and our solar system will one day come to an end – yes, even the sun will die one day. Then what? The miracle that is life will spring forth again, and again, and again, and all life springs forth from whence it came, from the realm where our ancestors await us, from the Source. If one day you pick up the newspaper or turn on the television and hear about a beautiful species of butterfly that has just become extinct, ask yourself, "Where did the butterfly go?" The answer is that the butterfly returned from whence it came. Just as you will, I will, we all will. We came forth, and we will return, just as the butterfly did. Many argue that the extinctions of the past were caused by cosmic events such as meteors striking the planet from afar and that today's extinctions are not natural as they can be directly attributed to the actions of humanity. However, when we say this and agree with this idea, we somehow remove humanity from the cosmos and the great wheel of life, as if our evolution of consciousness is somehow unnatural and does not belong in this world. If it doesn't belong here, then where does it belong? Just as our grandparents left in order to make room for us, and the dinosaurs left in order to make room for humanity, we cannot know the greater fate of humanity and our part in it, but we do know for sure that one day the sun will indeed die and all of us along with it. The sun, like each of us and the butterfly, will simply return from whence it came. None of this means that we as individuals are not required to respect nature and the life within it, or turn a blind eye when a property developer wishes to cut down a 400-year-old oak tree in order to build a car park, but in the greater scheme of things, the changes on planet earth today, whether environmental, political or social, are simply ripples in the fabric of evolutionary consciousness.

So why do anything at all, I hear you ask. The point to all of this is that, as we see the world as it is and acknowledge the workings of fate, we can have more time and energy for what really matters – the simplicity of love. And through our focus on what we love, we can heal the world one person at a time, starting with ourselves.

Allowing

Unfortunately, most of us give a lot of our energy to the resistance of what is. Giving up resistance and allowing really amount to the same thing. We look at the world and the people we interact with and, for the most part, we want the world and others to change. However, no matter how much we want others and the world to change, it simply remains out of reach, because our energy and focus are external rather that internal. When we are externally focused we want our sister not to be married to an abusive husband, and we don't want our good friend to be sick, or to smoke, and we don't want "those people" to be the way they are, or crime to be the way it is, or our mother to be the way she is or our partner to have certain habits. Much of the root of our unhappiness is simply resistance to what is. If we were to place as much energy and focus into creating what we want and into feeling good as we generally put into wanting others to change, our lives would be miraculously transformed. We are often stuck in the belief than in order to change the world we have to resist what is. This is often mirrored by society when we see campaigns that say such things as "War on Poverty", "Fight AIDS", "Campaign Against Violence". It seems curious that it is far easier to get us as individuals and groups to be against something rather than for it. Again, we have to look at our net contribution to the world, our friendships, relationships and family. If our contribution is more resistance, then nothing changes, for our energy and focus is then placed on that which we do not want, rather than on what we do want.

When individuals contemplate these principles for the first time, they often feel as if the principle is advocating apathy.

However, it is important to ask yourself, "Has my resistance to what is, actually changed anything at all, or does it simply make me feel frustrated, angry, sad or disappointed?" There is a principle that I have almost daily come across whilst working with others: most unhappiness stems from being involved in business that is not our own – be that our parent's marriage, our grandmother's unhappiness, our sibling's place in the world or our forming of opinions that have little to no basis in truth. In order to override these entanglements we need to get clear on whether something is our own business, someone else's, or that which falls into the realm of fate and therefore something over which we have absolutely no control.

When we allow others and the world to be what they are, even if those others are in unhappy marriages, ill, involved in drugs, crime, or sexual behaviour that does not conform to our own personal code of conduct, we relax and allow much more of our natural well-being to flow to us. We can get so tied up in the drama of life, taking on the problems of others as if they were our own, that we forget to live our own life and we allow our own dreams, aspirations and healing goals to slip by the wayside. Each of us is sovereign in our own world and our experience of it. Just as it may have taken effort on our part to make choices that are more supportive of who we want to be, we must likewise respect the choices and decisions of others. Allowing is one of the main keys to happiness – not only allowing ourselves to reach for more happiness and fulfillment but, equally importantly, allowing others the same, in their own unique ways. In order for us to achieve healing, more joy, more contentment and more fulfillment, no one else in the world needs to change. It is our very attention to the conditions in the world and the conditions that others live in or have created for themselves that slows up our progress, or halts it altogether. When we are in a state of allowing all that is, simply to be, we accelerate our path towards healing and creating a better life for ourselves. As we do this, we become a way-shower, not in terms of taking it upon ourselves to offer advice around our new-found freedom when it has not been asked for, but in terms of simply being with our new way of thinking, being and doing. The greatest gift we can give to others is to be at peace with the world. This has a far greater impact on others than resisting all that we see "wrong" with the world and other people's lives.

For example, let's say that your father is an alcoholic. You could choose to resist that fact and hold your entire life and happiness hostage with a state of disallowing around his alcoholism. You could even consciously be saying to yourself, "I cannot be happy until my father has given up alcohol". When we become so entangled in the affairs of another, we become the second addict in the scenario. Firstly, our father is addicted to alcohol, and secondly, we ourselves become addicted to the emotions surrounding the resistance to what is, and addicted to the resistance itself. When we make the choice to say, "My father is an alcoholic, and I love him anyway", resistance falls away. Yes, we do want him to live a better life, but is it our business to force that upon him? And when we get caught up in thoughts like, "But it makes my mother's life a misery", we are again becoming entangled in business that is not ours and there are a few things that we need to remind ourselves of. Firstly, no one can know the true nature of a couple relationship, except those who are in it. Secondly, these parents have chosen to remain together, and that is their choice.

When it comes to the world at large, allowing is a key principle not only for our own well-being, but also for the well-being of the planet. We may resist our government's actions in an overseas territory, or we may resist a certain ethnic or racial group for their behaviour. However, almost all of the world's problems are about one group of people disallowing another group of people their culture and way of life. When we tie up our energy and focus with these matters, all we are doing is adding to the growing level of disallowing in the world. In others words, we begin to disallow the disallowing of others.

The world is what it is, others are who they are, they do what they know to do, just as we ourselves do only what we know to do until such times as we learn something new. When we allow, we relax. It is important to respect not only the fate of others, but also their own way of solving problems, even if it seems as though they are not finding any solution. When we stick to that which is our business, we have much more time and energy for transforming ourselves. As each of us does this, the world is transformed, one person at a time. When we shout "World Peace", we usually mean that we want everybody else to think and behave in the same way that we do, and that just isn't possible. When we place our focus and energy into wanting everyone else to conform to our ideals, no matter how "right" or "good" they are, it is no different to the thinking of regimes that also seek to dominate and control others.

We cannot solve our problems with the
same thinking we used when we created them.

Albert Einstein

Defining What You Want

We can only ever truly have and create what we want for ourselves. Although we wish others well-being, good health and happiness, and it is totally natural to do so, we must ensure that our individual focus and attention is upon that which we are wanting ourselves – and without requiring a specific person to do that for us. When we place much energy on the thought, "I so want my mother to be happy", or, "I so want my friend Bob to be healthy", we take ourselves out of our own business into that of another. No one else needs to improve their lives in order for us to be happy. At times we can invest a lot in relationships where we become the rescuer, which only serves the purpose of taking us even further away from our happiness and goals in life. Likewise, we sabotage ourselves when we make our own happiness dependent on another person's loving us in the way in which we want them to. They will love us in the way that they can. Or not at all.

The world is at it is, and people are as they are. It is not that we shrug our shoulders and say that we no longer care or walk away if there is a cry for help. However, the essential message is this: others do not need to change one iota in order for us to be happy.

The world is at it is, and people are as they are.

Was es ist	What It Is
Es ist Unsinn	It is nonsense
sagt die Vernunft	says reason
Es ist was es ist	It is what it is
sagt die Liebe	says love
Es ist Unglück	It is misfortune
sagt die Berechnung	says calculation
Es ist nichts als Schmerz	It is nothing but pain
sagt die Angst	says fear
Es ist aussichtslos	It is hopeless
sagt die Einsicht	says insight
Es ist was es ist	It is what it is
sagt die Liebe	says love
Es ist lächerlich	It is ridiculous
sagt der Stolz	says pride
Es ist leichtsinning	It is careless
sagt die Vorsicht	says caution
Es ist unmöglich	It is impossible
sagt die Erfahrung	says experience
Es ist was es ist	It is what it is
sagt die Liebe	says love

by Erich Fried
Austrian Poet, 1921–1988

Translation by M. Kaldenbach

CHAPTER TWO

THE BURDENS OF GUILT AND REMORSE

Many of us are often burdened with feelings of guilt. Where does guilt come from? How can we tell the difference between guilt and remorse? Guilt is an emotion whose source is frequently unidentifiable, whereas remorse is directly linked to a particular act or a deed, or perhaps even to words that we have spoken. Guilt is also a different emotion to shame, although they are very closely linked.

Many clients over a period of several years have reported feelings of guilt, but on further investigation that is all it is, a feeling, not attached to any act or deed that produces a feeling of remorse. So where do these feelings come from, and how can we best deal with them? Is guilt ever appropriate, and what do we do with remorse?

Often when the difference between guilt and remorse is not understood, we find ourselves searching for logical reasons for our guilt and creating stories for ourselves in order to explain a feeling that we may have had our entire lives. When we do this, we may end up wasting many years nurturing or trying to solve a feeling of guilt that has no basis in truth and is not attached to a deed or words we have spoken. Does guilt come out of thin air, or does it have some other source?

Very often, as I work with others, a family sense of guilt is revealed, often carried by one individual that shoulders the feeling for the entire family system. Quite often, many individuals report feeling a sense of guilt but they are unable to pinpoint its source, simply feeling guilty for living a good life, or feeling that they don't deserve more.

How can we tell if our guilt is personal or if it stems from the family system? One of the easiest ways to know this is when we understand the difference between guilt and remorse, a distinction that many of us confuse. Remorse is as a result of something that we know we have done; it is attached to an event, a deed, or a specific relationship. Guilt, on the other hand, often unidentifiable in terms of its source, is simply a feeling.

Remorse is a very strong feeling. When remorse has been felt by a parent, grandparent or even great-grandparent, a feeling of guilt can be passed down through the family system for several generations. Quite often, when a sibling dies or is incapacitated in some way through illness or a chronic condition at a young age, the living siblings feel guilty for living, feeling that in some way they must "live less" in order to compensate for the one who has suffered. In such cases, we know that this is guilt, not remorse, assuming the sibling died of natural causes.

What kinds of events can lead to a sense of guilt that passes through many generations?

- When a woman dies in childbirth
- As a result of ill-gotten gain (wealth created out of greed, mistreatment of others or illegal activity)
- When a child has died as a result of negligence or cruelty
- Adoption
- Abortion (circumstance dependent)
- When marriages or engagements are ended owing to cultural pressures or in a disrespectful manner
- When a family member is forgotten or cast out
- Apartheid – African slavery – the Holocaust – Native American genocide
- Loss of a twin, Vanishing Twin Syndrome

When we have feelings of guilt that we cannot relate to remorse, these feelings are usually trans-generational in nature, or they spring forth as a result of our having been shamed in one way or another.

Each of us belongs to a family system that spans many generations. From an energetic point of view, each of us has what have been identified as "relationship cords" that emanate from our chakras and connect us to our intimate partners, parents, siblings, grandparents and distant ancestors. These cords give us a sense of belonging to those individuals. When the cords are damaged in some way, we may have a sense of not belonging to the family or even to this world. In addition to a feeling of belonging (or not belonging), feelings and emotions are communicated along these cords. Even the traumas of past generations can be felt as if they were our own. What has been observed is that the events of the past, when not resolved by the individuals involved, are simply transmitted along these cords to the next generation. For example, if your grandmother gave up a child for adoption, her feelings of remorse can remain within the family energy field and are felt by later generations as guilt, whether or not the later generations are fully cognisant of the story or the facts. Whenever an individual has been forgotten or cast out of a family, or an injustice has not been owned by the perpetrator, then a feeling of guilt will permeate an entire family system, or land on the shoulders of one or two individuals, often two to three generations later. As individuals, we are not islands, but we belong to a family "soul" or energy field that spans several generations, in which all feelings and experiences are contained.

One of the underlying principles of the soul is this: that which has been excluded will be included. For example, if your grandmother had a teenage pregnancy and was forced by her parents, owing to cultural shame, to give that child up for adoption, then her child has been excluded from the family soul. Yet the child belongs to the family soul irrespective of the decisions and feelings of the adults concerned. In such cases, when an individual is either excluded or ousted in this way, a vacuum is created and, as with all vacuums, something – or in this case someone (one or more) – is pulled into that vacuum. The person(s) pulled in will represent the missing child and the forced adoption, a generation or more later. When such events take place, there are many associated feelings: grief, remorse, anger, shame, exclusion, feelings of not belonging, etc. However, these feelings when felt across several generations can translate into nonspecific feelings of guilt, sadness or anger.

One of the challenges with such trans-generationally transmitted feelings is that we can fall into the trap of creating stories to fit our feelings, one of the great pitfalls of psychotherapy and other healing modalities. For example, our life may be dominated by the feeling of guilt (a false emotion). As there may be no event in our life that would cause us to have the feeling of remorse (a real emotion), in order to satisfy the demands of our intellect we then need to fit the emotion with a story. With this intellectual demand, we will then scan our memory banks and find incidents in our life that fit the emotion. When we do this, these incidents and the emotion of guilt (or any other emotion) become part of our "story". As time goes by, we nurture our story and it becomes larger, more significant, and eventually part of our identity and even our belief systems, which in turn mould and shape our reality. However, our stories are very subjective and are often devoid of factual evidence.

When we enter into the world of trans-generational healing, we soon learn that we are truly not individuals, islands in the midst of humanity, but rather we are one part of a greater whole, the greater whole of our biological family that stretches back several generations. The events of the past, be they wars, trauma, abortion, injustices, tragic deaths, family secrets or early deaths, all have an impact on our emotional make-up today. When we are burdened by feelings of guilt, it behooves us to ask ourselves whether the feeling is guilt or remorse. If it is remorse, then we can do something with it by looking at what we have done and finding a resolution to it. However, if it is guilt and there is no remorse, we need to understand that the feeling is likely not even our own and is therefore a false emotion. Many have asked me if such feelings of guilt can come from a past life. In my experience, all such feelings can be found within our family system, and resolution can be found through trans-generational healing.

Understanding the difference between guilt and remorse assists in bringing the presence of the soul closer to us. Guilt is a wasted emotion that we will simply create a story around, thereby moving out of alignment with simple truths and therefore the presence of our soul. Acknowledging remorse, and owning and/or rectifying that for which we are responsible, will bring us closer to the presence of our soul. The soul does not explain, "I did this to you because I was feeling this or that, and this other thing was going on in my life"; the soul simply says, "I am deeply sorry for wronging you in this way and I accept the consequences".

Artificial Guilt and Remorse – A Life Script

Whilst I was writing this book, a very dear friend called me in tears to say that he had just ended his relationship with his partner of two years. His tears were more about his sense of guilt than about the ending of the relationship. As we spoke, he explained that his partner was HIV positive, had no permanent full-time work and also no family anywhere near where they lived. I explained to him that he was not obliged to remain in a relationship that did not harmonize with him intellectually, spiritually or emotionally. His only reply was, "I feel like such a bad person for doing this". Knowing that his father died when he was eleven years old, I asked him if he had felt responsible for making his widowed mother happy in the years after that. He answered in the affirmative. I also asked him, now that his mother had re-married and her husband was an alcoholic, did he still feel the same? He answered in the affirmative. As we talked, I took him through the process of understanding the difference between guilt and remorse. He had not done anything to be remorseful of; he clearly was not responsible for his mother's life for he is only her son, and he simply does not have the power to determine his partner's destiny and life choices. Guilt often becomes the shackles that keep us enslaved to relationships that do not serve our greater good or our well-being. It became clear to my friend that his guilty feeling towards his mother and feeling responsible for her had become a life script, upon which most of his other relationships had become based.

The Hidden Self-Importance behind Guilt

As is clear with the story of my dear friend, his guilt revealed a hidden sense of self-importance. In making himself responsible for his mother's happiness, he was assuming that he was more capable than she was of creating her happiness. As children, how can we assume that we have that power, no matter our age? Likewise with a partner's happiness. When we feel guilty about the life and destiny of another, we assume that they are incapable of creating their own destiny, whilst at the same time assuming our own importance. We are simply not that powerful or important. The only thing that we ever have any real influence over is our own destiny and our own feelings; we cannot do that for another, nor should we assume that it is our job to do so. In essence, guilt can be a mask for arrogance and presumptuousness.

Feelings of guilt can also be indications of hidden loyalties. (See Chapter Three.)

Shame

Guilt can also arise out of having been shamed in some way. This could be as a result of sexual, verbal or physical abuse. When the shaming takes place, we receive the message that we are in some way wrong, bad, or simply not good enough, and guilt ensues. However, the difference between this kind of guilt and trans-generational guilt is that there is a process with the former in which we choose a belief that leads to guilt. When trans-generational guilt is present, we simply absorb the feeling without its being attached to an event about which we have made a decision. It is also important to state here that parents or others that shame their children are not free of shame themselves; therefore, irrespective of events, the feeling is already present within the family. As children we are psychic sponges who feel and sense all of the emotions and dominant thoughts present in the family, whether or not they are being expressed. In fact, it is evident that feelings and beliefs that are suppressed, or never discussed, are felt even more keenly by children. Again, this is testimony to the universal principle: That which is included will be represented – in other words, what we resist persists. As children we will live out any and all feelings that are held by our parents as if they are their own.

When we feel shamed in one way or another, we conclude that we are not being loved for who we really are, but being loved for what we are pretending to be. This often becomes a life-long pattern and we continue feeling unloved, all the while feeling a sense of guilt and shame for who we really are. When we live our lives in this way, behind the mask of trying to be that which we believe another will approve of, we lose contact with our essence and with the presence of our soul.

CHAPTER THREE

UNCOVERING HIDDEN LOYALTIES

A couple of years ago I very proudly went along to a car dealership to buy myself the most expensive and luxurious car I had ever owned. I was feeling very good and proud of myself and delighted that I would finally own a car that felt good for my body and personal comfort. As I approached the car, suddenly all of my good feeling went, as I heard an inner voice say, "You can't have a more expensive car than your father drives". I stopped in my tracks, completely stunned, wondering where on earth that thought and idea had sprung from. Over the years, I have observed that it often takes a very courageous person to live a better, happier and healthier life than their parents and grandparents did. Irrespective of whatever issues we may have with them on the personality level, our loyalty to them and their suffering knows almost no bounds. When it comes to the pursuit of money, we are often driven to create wealth in order to take care of others, or we sabotage the wealth creation process in order to remain loyal to the suffering of others. In other words, the false emotion of guilt, rather than the real feeling of remorse, becomes our measure for what we can and cannot have.

I saw my father experience great financial difficulties as I entered my teenage years and, during a period of a couple of very bad years, I saw him work extremely long hours in jobs that didn't suit him, just to be able to put food on the table and keep a roof over our heads. I was also very aware of the childhoods that both of my parents had had, marred by the Second World War in Europe. My inner feeling was that it would be unfair on them if my life were easy and if good things came to me without much effort, as they had had to work so hard for everything. Hence, a hidden loyalty was revealed as I approached my large, shiny, luxurious car. What was further revealed was the source of my guilt for wanting my life to be easy or abundant, and also a hidden arrogance. Who was I to dictate what my parents wanted for my life? Who was I to decide that by limiting my life it would in some way make their lives happier? To the contrary, every parent I know is celebratory of their child's successes and actually wants their child, no matter the age, to be more abundant, successful, healthier and happier than they were! I have learnt that when we make our life small, or allow it to be less than we truly want it to be, out of loyalty to those that have had difficult and challenging times, we denigrate the life that has been given to us.

Hidden loyalty to a mother's or father's suffering is relatively easy to identify. However, in the process of my work with clients, we have uncovered loyalties that can span generations and are, for the most part, completely unconscious.

Sharon

Sharon came to me in order to find resolution around a pattern she had identified with the men she had dated. She reported that each time she started to fall in love with a man, he ended the relationship. She was feeling hurt, angry and confused as to why she always seemed to choose the "wrong men". As we worked together in taking her family history, she revealed that her grandmother had been deeply in love with a handsome young sea captain who had been lost at sea. Her grandmother subsequently married her grandfather, eventually resulting in the Sharon we see today. I asked her to visualize her grandmother and to tell me what she was feeling. She reported feeling sad, but also happy to see her. I then asked her to imagine that the handsome young sea captain was standing next to her grandmother. Tears began to roll down her cheeks. "What is making you sad?" I enquired. She told me that she felt it was very sad that her grandmother had lost the man that she was so much in love with. I then asked her to become fully aware of her body's responses when I gave her the sentence, "Out of loyalty to you, dear Grandmother, I too will not have my great love". Sharon visibly shook, opened her eyes, and wept some more. "That's it!" she exclaimed. "I was always aware as a child that my grandmother was unhappy in some way and I had the feeling of wanting to help her, or to make her happy". I then asked her if she thought it would make her grandmother happy if she were to suffer the same or a similar fate. As we worked, Sharon was able to understand that her loyalty to her Grandmother was a disservice, rather than a service. She also realized that she had made herself far too important and what was required was to bow deeply in respect to her grandmother's fate – for, after all, had the young sea captain not gone missing, Sharon, her mother, and her grandfather would not be! This is the power of fate and it is not ours to question how or why; fate simply is.

Traditional psychotherapy may have taken Sharon on a journey to explore her own commitment issues, intimacy and also her relationship to her parents. When the power of hidden loyalties is not known or understood, however, then great stories can be created in order to explain such patterns. Sharon could have decided that her father did not show his love to her, and therefore she was caught up in this repeating pattern of choosing men that would do the same, demonizing her father in the process, which in turn could result in even more therapy around the "issue" of her father.

Prem

Similarly, I worked with a young woman of Indian descent called Prem. She had witnessed her mother being beaten by her father over many years. Prem said that she had a wonderful husband who was gentle, kind, generous and handsome on top of it all. However, Prem was unhappy and reported that she seemed to be complaining about her husband a lot, shouting at him, and once she physically attacked him. The marriage had broken down so far that her husband was now talking of divorce. "Why am I doing this?" she asked. Many therapists would answer that she attacked her husband because her father through his actions had taught her that this was appropriate behaviour. However, whilst this may be a learned response, there was a far deeper truth. I asked Prem to choose someone from the workshop to represent her mother and then got her to stand beside her mother and simply to look at her. "How does she seem?" I enquired. "She looks unhappy", Prem told me. The next movement was to ask Prem to say the following to her mother: "Mother, I don't yet have the courage to be happier than you". Prem started to cry. "It's so true", she declared, "I feel guilty for having such a good husband so I'm trying to get rid of him!" A deep realization sank in for Prem in that moment of stating what is. In order to start the healing of her detrimental loyalty to her mother, I next had Prem say, "Please bless me if I have the courage to be happier than you, dear mother".

Prem felt relieved. Just three weeks later she reported that her husband was no longer speaking of divorce and that she continued to work on allowing her own happiness even though her mother was deeply unhappy. Another vital ingredient of our work together was to point out to Prem that her mother had a choice, and that to date her mother had chosen to remain with her husband and that that was none of Prem's concern. In essence, as I mentioned in the beginning of this book, Prem was entangled in another person's business. Her mother's choices and unhappiness were indeed only her mother's business and not Prem's at all.

Again we see that even hidden loyalties, although an act of love, are in fact instances of being entangled in the fate of another and making it our own business.

Matthew

Matthew reported that his life was simply not working for him. He had had many jobs and periods of unemployment, financial difficulties and relationships that did not last long. In essence, Matthew was feeling that his life was a mess and not going anywhere. After a few short questions regarding Matthew's family history, he revealed to me that he had been conceived as a twin. He knew this as his parents had told him that when his mother was pregnant with him she had had a suspected miscarriage in the third month and that the doctors had told her that she had probably lost a twin. I asked Matthew to get very quiet and to become aware of his breathing. "Do you have a sense of a brother or a sister?" I enquired. "A brother, definitely a brother", Matthew replied with a tear rolling down his cheek. I asked another young man in the workshop to come and stand in front of Matthew and represent his lost twin brother. "How do you feel when you see him?" I asked.

"Sad, very sad, but also guilty", replied Matthew.

"Please tell me about your feelings of guilt", I asked.

"It should have been me. It is not fair that he died and that I live", answered Matthew.

"So now we know why your life is not working for you. You are sabotaging your happiness out of loyalty to your brother", I offered.

I asked Matthew to stand next his brother and the two young men looked at each other intently. "How are things when you look at him so closely?" I enquired.

"Strangely, more relaxed, less guilty than before", Matthew responded.

I then asked Matthew to look at his brother and say, "Dear Brother, I have missed you dearly. Please smile upon me kindly if I have the courage to live a happy life".

With this simple but very deep process, Matthew was able to release much deeply-held emotion and he felt a great sense of relief as he asked his brother to smile upon him kindly. When others have suffered it is often very important to inwardly ask for their blessing if we want to have the courage to lead happy and fulfilled lives. For Matthew, this would be an ongoing process, one of moving through various layers of grief, guilt and the natural longing he would feel for his twin. An important aspect of this inner work is to both acknowledge and respect the fate of another. What is very important to point out here is that Matthew's twin was miscarried in the first trimester and therefore the loss is something that Matthew himself was not conscious of until we started our work together. Many of us can easily accept that, should we lose a twin when a child or a teenager, these feelings would be natural and normal; however, few of us suspect that the feelings can be just as alive and dominant when the loss occurs prior to birth and we have no conscious memory of it. My work has shown me that loyalties even to the unborn can and indeed do exist.

Sophia

Sophia was a very beautiful, artistic woman in her mid-thirties who reported that life was one long struggle with one disappointment after the other.

"Nothing ever works for me, it is like there is a curse on my life", Sophia explained. "I always get involved with the wrong types of guys, my career in the arts has just been one disappointment after the other, I struggle financially and bad luck seems to follow me everywhere I go".

"That's quite a lot of unhappiness you are dealing with there, but let us investigate", I replied.

Sophia recounted that before she had been born her mother had had three abortions. I randomly chose three individuals to represent her three aborted siblings. Sophia broke down and began to shake a little.

"What is happening?" I asked.

"It's terrible, I feel so guilty", she replied.

I went on to say, "Please say to them, 'Your fate belongs with our mother'".

Sophia felt very resistant to saying this and, as our discussion ensued, it was revealed that she felt compelled to do something in order to put this right. "So you are suffering on behalf of them, as if that will change something? Or are you paying a sort of a penance for your mother?" I asked.

Next I asked her to imagine saying to her mother, "It is none of my business and I leave this with you", and she felt a sense of relief. The next step was to ask her to look at her aborted siblings and say, "My fate was different, please smile upon me kindly if I have the courage to life a full life".

There were two very important elements to this issue that Sophia was able to resolve. Firstly, she understood that the fate of the children lies with her mother and therefore has nothing to do with her, and, secondly, that living a difficult life did not honour her siblings at all. She felt relief on both counts: by respectfully leaving the guilt with her mother to whom it belonged, and by understanding that mimicking the fate of her siblings through limiting her life did not honour them.

Robert

"I am all alone", said Robert. "I have few friends, spend much of my time alone, and never have relationships".

"Who else was 'all alone' in your family?" I asked.

"My grandfather, I guess. He was raised in an orphanage after his parents died tragically", replied Robert.

I asked Robert to imagine that his grandfather was standing in front of him. He reported feeling very sad as he did so and said that the very well-known feeling of being "all alone" became stronger as he did so. I asked Robert to say, "Dear Grandfather, I have carried these feelings out of love for you". Robert was deeply moved and shed a tear. I then asked him to say, "Dear Grandfather, please bless me if I have the courage to be happier than you". Robert initially felt some resistance, but after I asked him to include his grandfather's parents into his image he relaxed and was able to say the sentence again.

Gloria

Gloria was a hard-working African-American woman and a single mother of three children.

"My life is so hard. I work long hours and struggle to make ends meet. I have three children from two different fathers who simply left. Everything is so difficult and I cannot see a way out of my difficult life; it often feels like it is too much", Gloria shared.

I asked Gloria to imagine that there were two women standing in front of her, both of whom were her ancestors and were also African slaves. Gloria began to weep and said, "I love them so much, and they suffered terribly".

I asked Gloria to say the following to them: "I have loved you so much that I am willing to suffer as you did". With those words the collective grief of African-American slavery rose up within Gloria as she wept for herself and for her ancestors. "You see, my dear", I offered, "you have created a life of slavery and bondage out of loyalty to them".

"I have", replied Gloria. "My life feels like slavery, all I do is work, work, work and get nowhere. But I cannot be disloyal to them".

"What would give their souls more peace?" I asked. "That you continue to live as a slave out of loyalty to them, or that you honour their fate and their courage by living a full life?"

"I've never seen it that way. I accepted suffering as my lot in life", Gloria replied.

I then asked Gloria to say to her ancestors, "You survived in order to pass on life to me. Thank you for that. Now I shall honour you by living my life more fully. Please bless me if I have the courage to do so".

Gloria felt great relief and she felt a rush of new energy running through her body as she uttered these words.

It has been revealed that hidden loyalties can span many generations – so much so that, when we try to uncover disruptive life patterns, it is often very difficult for us to pinpoint the origin of the loyalty. Instead, we focus on what we know and on what we can remember, often explaining our disruptive life patterns with stories of our parents and early childhood. Whilst it is true that some experiences in childhood can and do assist in the formation of disruptive life patterns and limiting belief systems, they are not the complete story. It is more often than not a hidden loyalty that is the originating factor. Some loyalties are clear to see, such as an individual's loyalty to a hard-working single mother, or a loyalty to a beleaguered community or ethnic group, but others can be so hidden that they at first can be difficult to identify when we don't understand the trans-generational nature of family consciousness. Some loyalties even extend beyond the family. Let me give you an example.

Suzanne

"I've been dating a young black man for about two years. Our relationship is not good or even satisfying. He is at a different educational level, we argue a lot, and he has even hit me a few times, and yet I feel compelled to continue seeing him".

When Suzanne used the word "compelled", I knew that there was a hidden loyalty and perhaps even some event in her family that had in some way affected a black family. As we investigated her family, she told me that her father had at one time been a member of the AWB*, an extreme right-wing political organization that is racist to the core. Her parents were farmers and had many black labourers and domestic workers on their farm during the apartheid years in South Africa.

I asked her to imagine a group of black labourers and domestic workers that had worked for her parents when she was a child. She began to weep and also reported that she was feeling very angry, even enraged. "It's so wrong!" she exclaimed. "They were treated so badly!" As we continued to work it became clear to Suzanne that her compulsion to date the man that she was clearly unhappy with was directly linked to her loyalty to those who had been treated so unjustly. She also realized that not only was she offering a disservice to the young man in question, for her bond with him was not based on affection, but she was also entangled in business that belonged to her father and not to her. I took Suzanne through another process in which she was able to understand the difference between guilt and remorse. When we experience feelings of guilt, it invariably has nothing to do with us but belongs to another. She began to understand that remorse is attached to actual personal deeds and that guilt is simply a feeling; in her case, the feelings of remorse belonged to her father's soul, and not to her. She ended the relationship within a few days of our process together.

In order to assist you in the process of uncovering hidden loyalties, I've put together the following exercise:

---

* AWB. Afrikaanse Weerstands Beweging – Afrikaner Resistance Movement.

Exercise: Important Questions

Before answering the following questions, ensure that you will not be disturbed for several minutes. Relax, become aware of your body and take a few deep breaths. When you feel centered, ask yourself each of the following questions one by one, giving pause between them so that you can gauge your response.

Do I have the courage to be happier than my mother?

Do I have the courage to be happier than my father?

Do I have the courage to be happier than my brother?

Do I have the courage to be happier than my sister?

If you have an emotional response or even a direct "No", then imagine that the individual in question is standing right in front of you, and say:

"Dear Mother, please bless me if I have the courage to be happier than you".

Or:

"Dear Father, please smile upon me kindly if I have the courage to be happier than you".

Once you've asked yourself the question regarding each member of your immediate family, take a few moments to remember or to note down any specific individuals in your family that you know to have suffered. Some examples:

- *Your grandmother who had a stillborn child*
- *Members of your mother's family who died in the Holocaust*
- *Your close friend/brother/cousin who died in a car accident*
- *Your ancestors who were African slaves*
- *Your sister who has breast cancer*
- *Your grandfather who was raised in an orphanage*
- *Members of the family who suffered during World War II, the American Civil War, the sectarian violence in Northern Ireland, the clan wars of Scotland, etc.*

Once you've remembered those who have suffered, repeat the exercise above. Those that have stimulated the strongest response are the ones you need to focus on. Our loyalty to those who have suffered can be far stronger than we could have ever imagined. When we acknowledge their fate with deep respect, we can also inwardly ask for their blessing.

The important thing to realize is that these loyalties do not serve either ourselves or those to whom we are loyal. For the most part, those to whom we are loyal have long ago passed on. Just as we would not want others to suffer on our behalf, neither do they. Identifying and releasing hidden loyalties is an important aspect of our inner work, for when we have done so, we can more easily live the life we are meant to live, one that is blessed by abundance in all of its forms.

Loyalty to those who have suffered is deeply entrenched in western culture in the form of Christian belief and doctrine. We are taught about the suffering of Jesus for our sins and many of the images that Christianity portrays are those of the suffering martyrs. In essence, we have been taught that to suffer out of loyalty to others is a path towards redemption. Our Christian teachings are replete with sentences such as, "For God so loved the world that he gave his only begotten son", and the notion that another is able to die for our sins. Although we may have the personal conviction that we are not religious, it is important to understand that such notions have been passed down through many generations and that the beliefs are deeply engrained.

When working to assist individuals to divest themselves of loyalties that are counter-productive, many report feelings of betrayal, feeling that they are in some way betraying others that have suffered. When we look at indigenous nations such as the Maori of New Zealand, the Australian Aboriginals, Native Americans and Black South Africans in urban communities, we often see high rates of alcoholism, drug addiction and unemployment. It is clear that these individuals are not only mourning the loss of their tribes and large parts of their culture, but are also loyal to those that suffered cruelly at the hands of European settlers. Thankfully, today in many of the former colonies there is a renaissance of indigenous culture and language, once again bringing a sense of pride to these dispossessed peoples. Similarly, we see the revival of native language and culture in many parts of Europe – Wales, Catalonia and Bretagne, for example. These areas of Europe have long been dominated by the larger European nations such as England, Spain and France. This renaissance is an integral part of the healing process for individuals and nations.

William

William was a tall, imposing man in his fifties who attended a workshop in Scotland. I noticed that underneath his mirth and wit there seemed to be an underlying anger, for many of his quips and jokes were directed at the English in attendance at the workshop. When we worked together, the first thing he identified was his anger and he shared that it had been the dominant emotion throughout his life.

Following an inspired thought, I asked a man in the workshop to stand in front of William. In my mind, this man represented Sir William Wallace, a Scottish nobleman who fought for the independence of Scotland from England. He had been betrayed by a Scottish knight in service to the English king, arrested near Glasgow and executed in brutal and cruel fashion. My client William had no idea who he was looking at, but simply my intention to represent an important historical Scottish figure was sufficient to reveal the hidden loyalties and the anger associated with them. William reported feeling not only more anger, but also a deep grief. He shed tears and said, "I know these feelings, but who is this man?" I asked him to wait a while before I revealed the story. I next took another to represent the Scottish nobleman that had betrayed Wallace and yet another to represent King Edward of England. William reported feeling even more anger and rage and at this point I revealed the story I had set up with the representatives. As William wept, I said to him, "You are angry about the betrayal of your people and the subjugation of the Scots by the English, that is very clear to see". A gentle discussion ensued in which I pointed out to him that his continued anger at the atrocities from so many centuries before no longer served him as an individual, his ancestors, nor his beloved Scotland. William pointed out that his two sons have married English women. I smiled at him, saying, "And so we have it, the universal principle of inclusion: that which is excluded will be included by another".

Is it really possible that we as individuals can carry loyalties concerning events that stretch back to the 13th and 14th centuries, and live out those emotions as if they are our own? The short answer is yes. Growing up I became very aware of the deeply ingrained mistrust between the English and the French. The French were often derided and labelled as traitors and as a nation that could not be trusted, much of this being explained by their actions during World War II. However, the more I observed the transgenerational impact of historical events, the more I realized that there was more to the mistrust between these two nations than at first is apparent. The two nations' history with one another is long and often bloody. There was the invasion of England in 1066 by William of Normandy in which the Saxon king, Harold, was killed; the Hundred Years' War and the execution of Jean d'Arc, now the patron saint of France; and then the influx of French Huguenots, French protestants who had suffered great atrocities under French Catholics, into southern England. The memories and the feelings are embedded deep within the souls of both of these nations, each feeling the trauma and the pain of the past, and each still loyal to those that suffered. Despite the fact that these two nations are now great allies in a greater European Union, the underlying feelings remain, not only within the nations themselves, but also within many individuals.

What is important to remember is that whilst we are members of a family, we are also members of greater families that we call nations, ethnic groups and defined cultures. Additionally, whilst we may dismiss a war that took place some three or five hundred years ago as having any relevance, we must remember that it is our ancestors who fought those wars and suffered the consequences of their actions and the actions of others. These events led to trauma, and trauma always has a deep residual impact that can span many generations. It is perhaps easier for us to conceptualize that if our great-grandmother's great love was lost at sea, or if our greatgrandfather was abandoned and left in an orphanage, we may feel their feelings and live them our as our own. It may be more difficult to grasp that we may have feelings and impulses that have their origins in the mists of time or are related to specific events that took place some five hundred years ago. My client William's feelings of anger are testimony to the trans-generational transference of trauma and the associated feelings.

What can we do about such feelings? When we are unaware of the importance of events that affected our ancestors, identifying the source of such feelings can become a little like a wild goose chase, for we need to create logical stories that fit with the emotion we are feeling or a belief that is holding us back. This can lead us to cling to memories of events from our childhood that explain the emotion or belief but in reality may have little to do with them – and so we become imprisoned within a story that becomes our script for life.

Honouring the Ancestors – Creating Your Sacred Space

Much is misunderstood in the Christian world regarding the practice of honouring the ancestors in African, Native American and other indigenous cultures. Praying to the ancestors is not a form of worship, but rather a request for the ancestors' blessings and giving them thanks for the life that we have. Each of these cultures reveres a "Great Spirit" or "God" and the ancestors are seen either as a go-between or as individuals that are closer to that Great Spirit than we are in the physical world.

It is important to remember that it is the dreams, aspirations, striving and hard work of our ancestors that have made possible the life we lead today. In creating our altar, we not only respect the fate of those that suffered; we also ask for the strength and wisdom that our ancestors hold.

Creating Your Altar

Find a wonderful space in your home and dedicate it to being a sacred space. This could be your mantelpiece, a special table, or a corner in one of your favourite rooms. You may wish to drape this area with a special cloth of high quality, such as pure cotton or silk.

Things to place on your altar:

- Photos of parents, grandparents and great grandparents
- A candle
- A semi-precious or polished stone to represent your distant ancestors (e.g., quartz, amethyst, river pebble, etc.)
- Incense or a smudge stick.

If you do not have photos of your grandparents or great grandparents, you may represent each of them individually with a polished stone, river pebble or semi-precious stone.

You may also wish to represent your ancestors' culture and religion in some way – Star of David, Greek Orthodox cross, map of Africa, beads, a thistle to represent Scotland, a Chinese good luck symbol, or a blessing written in the language of your ancestors if it is different to the one you as their descendant speak today. If you are in the United States, Canada, South Africa, New Zealand, South America, or Australia, it is quite likely that your ancestors originate from different parts of the world and represent more than one culture. Whilst it is important to honour your heritage, do not become overly concerned at finding symbols for each of the cultures they represent.

Special Note: If your ancestor's culture uses ritualistic masks (African, Indonesian, etc.), it is important only to use masks that have been passed down through your family. Masks are generally made for ceremonial purposes, often to ward off evil spirits and at times for black magic. I do not recommend placing these masks on your altar as they can harbour unwanted energies.

Blessing Corner

On your altar, create a blessing corner to represent the perpetrators and victims of the past. For example:

- If you are African-American, represent the descendants of the slave traders and masters, as well as the slaves themselves

- If you are Jewish, represent the descendants of the Germans, the Nazis or those that led the pogroms, as well as the Jews
- If you are German, represent your country's Nazi history, the Jews, the Poles, etc.

It is important that neither the persecutors nor the victims in our ancestry be excluded, and in prayer we can ask that our ancestors bless the descendants of their persecutors. For example, if your grandfather was murdered, you can also represent the family of the murderer and ask them to be blessed and free of the guilt caused by their family member.

You may also wish to offer up any of the following healing sentences that are appropriate to you:

"Please bless me if I have the courage to be happier than those who have suffered".

"Beloved Ancestors, please bless those that hurt you, and their children and children's children for all generations, so that we may be at peace with them".

"Beloved Ancestors, please assist me to give a place in my heart to the slave masters, their children and their children's children, so that I may be at peace with them".

"Beloved German brothers and sisters, I give your people a place in my heart, along with your children and your children's children for many generations to come".

Meditation

Find a time, whenever it feels appropriate, be that once in a while, every week or every day, to sit in contemplation, meditation or prayer before your ancestral altar. Below are some guidelines and suggestions for your spiritual practice.

Forgiveness versus Blessing

It is not our place to forgive the perpetrators of the past or to ask forgiveness of the victims of our ancestors, for that would be interfering in their business. Furthermore, offering forgiveness is often done from a place of superiority. Simply asking that they be blessed is sufficient.

You may also wish to ask your ancestors to bless your children and grandchildren and ask that they be freed from the burdens of the past.

Request for Healing

During your meditation, ask that you be released from any suffering that you may be carrying on behalf of anyone else. When you do this, know that you can entrust it to the soul of your ancestor (known or unknown) who will assist those that suffered in carrying their own fate.

Offer Gratitude

You may wish to bring an offering to place on your altar as a symbol of your gratitude to those that came before. In some cultures, it is believed that fruits and money can be used in the afterlife by the ancestors. However, as the ancestors have no need of physical items, these items can represent your own prosperity and be offered up in gratitude.

You may wish to offer gratitude for:

- The opportunity to live in these times
- Life itself
- The knowledge, experience and wisdom passed down through the generations and ancestral memory
- The gifts and traditions of your ancestor's culture
- The opportunity to live as a citizen of your current country, if your ancestors arrived in the country where you live from elsewhere.

This simple but reverent process of approaching your ancestors through an altar dedicated to them can be very healing, whether this is done once or on a regular basis. Choose your own time and enter into this ritual as often as it feels good for you to do so.

Living Loyalties

Through thick and thin, a child is invariably loyal to its parents, even when parents have been abusive and have caused physical harm. It is the most natural thing in the world for a child at any age to be loyal to those that gave them life, and society also impresses upon us that a good child is loyal to his or her mother and father. When we are criticized or hurt in some way by our parents, we will live out their criticism of us out of loyalty. If we are told that we will never amount to anything, this is what we will do in one or many areas of our life. If we are told that we are not good at a particular thing, we will probably never develop that skill and overcome our identified shortcoming, out of loyalty to our parents. In essence, out of loyalty to those that gave us life, we will live out whatever it is that they have told us, either directly or indirectly. So many of the messages we receive as children are non-verbal, but as children we are psychic sponges that absorb virtually every belief, every sentiment and every emotion being expressed or repressed within our family system. If we come from a family that has many health issues, then we, too, are likely to develop health problems in order to belong. If we come from a family that struggled with money, then we, too, will often sabotage wealth in order to belong.

We will often habitually live out the statements, the proclamations and the beliefs that our family has offered us as its view of reality. However, as we have discovered with the trans-generational transference of beliefs and trauma, our parents are simply living out what they themselves received from their own families. Becoming conscious of these destructive loyalties will go a long way toward freeing yourself from the burden of living out something that is less than your greater self. The dilemma we face when we uncover such scripts from which we are playing out our lives is how to change them without feeling disloyal to our parents, siblings and ancestors. Becoming angry about the scripts we received does not help either, for we are placing blame on individuals that were blameless in that they, too, readily accepted the scripts from the generation before them, and so on. Freeing ourselves from the scripts is being able to acknowledge the good that was also passed down to us, starting with life itself. An inner statement would go something like this: "Dear Mother and Father, you gave me life freely and for that I am truly grateful. I now take you as my parents fully and will do something good with the life you have given me. With deep respect, I leave you with that which is yours".

As You Feel, I Will Do

Another aspect to loyalty is this: what a parent feels, a child will do. It follows the universal principle that that which is excluded will be represented or included in some way. Therefore, if your mother feels ugly and does not express it, you may not only feel ugly but also express it in an exaggerated way, for it would be disloyal if you were to feel attractive, handsome or pretty. If your father, despite being surrounded by people, feels lonely, you may live out his loneliness in an exaggerated way by living as a recluse. Parents often feel that they are protecting their children by not saying anything about how they really feel, believing somehow that what the child does not hear, the child will not know. However, it is simply not so. What is not said will be felt and understood very keenly by children. When the parent does not heal their own wound, it is simply passed on, often in an exaggerated form. It becomes exaggerated owing to the repression of the feeling for, as it is repressed, pressure mounts, sometimes over generations, until someone begins to live out the feelings fully. It is at this point that most parents look at their child with confusion, not understanding the problems that their child has. However, when we simply scratch the surface of our world of hidden feelings, it becomes clear that our child is simply doing what we are not saying and living out what we have not healed within ourselves.

Chapter Four

INHERITED BELIEF SYSTEMS

During the course of my work with many hundreds of individuals, I began to see patterns which begged some very important questions. Quite often a client of mine would explain to me that she had been sexually abused as a child or raped as an adult. When I investigated the family history of such individuals, they would very often reveal that their mother had had the same experience, along with their grandmother, their aunt, great-grandmother, and so on. Additionally, clients would tell me how they had moved from one abusive relationship to another and that their parent's marriage was also abusive – or that they had struggled with money all of their lives and that their grandfather had gone bankrupt. The stories continued and the evidence mounted. As previously discussed in this book, it became evident to me that there was more to these repeating patterns than just hidden loyalties to those who had suffered.

How is it that you can go out, meet a charming individual by pure chance, fall in love, get married, and then experience that this person is violent and abusive towards you? How is it that an innocent child can end up having the same experience as her mother and grandmother? How do we draw these experiences into our lives? It is pure coincidence, or is there something deeper at work here?

Over the years I have begun to understand that we live in a universe of energy and information and that this energy is a field of resonance. In the physical universe, science has explained to us how galaxies and suns and entire solar systems are created by the process of accretion. The process of accretion, or the Law of Increase, is the process whereby materials of a similar nature are attracted to one another. Gases are drawn to one another and gradually over time form the great balls of burning gas we know as our sun and the stars. Various elements are drawn together in order to form solid mass, which in turn forms rocks, which in turn are drawn to other rocks in order to form planets, including the one we call home, earth. As it is with everything in the universe, "as above, so below". Not only do we see the process of accretion in the physical world; it is also true for vibration, energy and experiences. That which is similar is magnetically drawn. Beyond the physical, each of us is an energy being and the primary energy that we exude into our world experience is the energy of our thoughts and emotions. Thoughts can be measured in terms of frequency. Repetitive thoughts and deeply-held beliefs emit a frequency and, as with everything else in the universe, they are magnetic to that which is similar. They, too, are part of the process of accretion; they activate the Law of Increase, also known as the Law of Attraction. That which we think, feel and believe becomes true in our experience.

Understanding the Law of Attraction gave me a key to understanding how it is that generations of women in one family can all have the same experience at the hands of different perpetrators in different locations and periods of time. I also began to understand how having a grandfather who went bankrupt can lead to our financial difficulties today. But how does this all work? Certainly most descendants of those upon whom a tragedy fell have not been actively thinking about bankruptcy, rape, illness, misfortune and abusive partners.

One Part of the Whole

As individuals, we are not islands; we belong to a family system or soul, a nation, an ethnic group, a religion, a race and a gender, all of which hold perceptions and beliefs about themselves, their place in the world and their fate. However, our main belonging is to our family system, which has a much greater impact on our life experience than even many psychologists understand.

Beyond the physical body, we are also energy beings possessing an emotional body, a mental body and a spiritual body. Beyond our five senses, we are also telepathic beings and we respond to the energies around us. The energies around us are created by the beliefs, emotions and intentions of those we come into contact with, and in childhood we absorb these like a sponge. Studies have shown that even in the womb we are very aware of the feelings and thoughts of both our mother and father. Most of us can clearly understand how we can absorb and feel the feelings of our mother, for we are within her body and travel with her everywhere she goes and, from a biological point of view, we are also exposed to any hormonal changes that she experiences as a result of strong emotion. How, then, are we influenced by our father? To put it simply, our physical body is 50% our father; his sperm cell is the other half of the life-creating process. Just as memories, feelings and emotions are stored in our physical bodies, they are "remembered" in each cell, and so it is with sperm cells. Hence, we inherit the emotional patterns and beliefs systems of our father, as well. Beyond that, energy healers have shown us that not only do we receive this package at conception; we continue to receive the father's non-verbal input throughout gestation and well into childhood.

This transference occurs through what have been described as energy cords that emanate from our non-physical bodies to our parents and to our more distant ancestors such as grandparents and great-grandparents. It is along these cords that telepathic communication takes place and through which beliefs and feelings are transferred. Furthermore, what is true for the individual is also true on the macro scale. Just as we individuals have an energy body made up of an emotional and mental body, so does the family system. In other words, the family "soul" has a collective emotional and mental body in which all the experiences are beliefs are stored, both positive and negative, along with unresolved trauma. As the universe is made up of energy and information, so is the family soul. The energy field of all families, spanning many generations, is replete with information, beliefs and emotional frequencies that we tap into from the moment of our conception. Many have assumed that those who cannot speak do not think and do not respond to thoughts that they are exposed to, but this is far from the truth. Generally, when we are worried about something, we are not having a dialogue of words in our head about the thing that is concerning us; we are simply feeling and experiencing a dominant thought that is not expressed in words. If you meditate on a regular basis, you will understand that you can be pondering a thought without having a conversation made up of words with yourself in your head, and so it is with us as pre-verbal children, even when in the womb.

Through my work, I have also witnessed that it is not only belief systems but also feelings and even memories that can be transferred from one generation to the next. In recent years there has been much discussion regarding False Memory Syndrome. During the 1990's many individuals in therapy were recovering suppressed memories of sexual abuse, and, as a result of this, many innocent men and women were falsely accused. What I have discovered is that many individuals that suspect or perhaps have the feeling of having been sexually abused as children are in fact tapping into the larger family emotional and mental field and are experiencing the result of events that took place one or more generations previously. Whilst it may be true that some therapists have been on a kind of witch hunt to root out sexual predators, this does not explain the entire story regarding False Memory Syndrome. What is clear to me is that if an individual – a mother or grandmother, for example – has experienced the trauma of sexual abuse, that trauma is very present within the greater family soul; the information, the images, the feelings and emotions are present enough for us not only to feel but also to recover as a memory as if it were our own. As our conscious mind does not understand the workings of the collective subconscious of the family, or the energetic memory transference of such events, it then needs to create a story to fit with the "evidence". The point to explaining all is this is to communicate that trauma has a deep residual impact that can span many generations – so much so that many traumas can be felt as if they are our own, and so we can easily reach conclusions and manifest beliefs that are created in the aftermath of trauma.

All of the evidence of my work has shown me that we are not islands, but simply a part of the whole. As we are a part of a family system, it means that we emerge into this world with feelings and beliefs that begin to mould our direct experience. In essence, if bankruptcy, sexual abuse, ill health or abusive relationships have been a part of our family's history, we are predisposed to creating those very experiences within our own life. If we look back far enough into any family history, all of the experiences of rape, murder, starvation, cruelty, poverty, disease and illness are true for every family on earth, even if those events occurred fifteen, twenty or thirty generations ago.

The belief that we create our own reality, and the understanding of The Law of Attraction, have been growing in acceptance and popularity over the past two decades or so. However, this is often taught, shared and communicated in a way that can make some individuals feel guilty for their own negative experiences. There are some who say that if you have been raped, or went bankrupt, then you must have brought it on yourself by thinking about it too much, or you have certain beliefs concerning money or the safety of women. This view lacks compassion, is ignorant of the bigger picture, and only serves to add guilt to the trauma. Whilst there is some truth in this, such sentiments lack the deeper understanding of the nature of thought and emotional centering as inherited from our family system. Some only see inherited beliefs as coming from the time that their mother or father criticized them for not doing something well, and now they do not "believe in themselves" and so they cannot achieve success in one field or another. It goes far beyond that, in my experience. Although we do pick up thoughts along the way, and make certain decisions regarding the nature of our world and what is true, for the most part, our perceptions, beliefs and many of our feelings are present well before we exit the womb or are able to utter a single word. In addition to the thoughts, feelings and beliefs we inherit, we must also take into consideration hidden loyalties.

Beliefs Resulting from Trauma

Whilst it is relatively easy to accept the evidence that if a trauma befell our grandfather or great-grandmother then those feelings and the resulting beliefs are transferred to us, which can directly influence and create our own experience. The next questions is: How did it happen to them?

To understand this, we also need to look at the evolution of human consciousness and the nature of the soul. We must consider the non-physical part of us that emerged into this physical world. As non-physical beings we left a world that was limitless and entered a world that seemed limited by virtue of its physicality. We began to perceive the mortality of our physical bodies, the limitations of the world we lived in; everything seemed to have a finite measure. The land we lived on had a certain size, the amount of food available was limited by the environment, and, most of all, we felt limited by our physical body. It could feel pain, it died, it could be injured and it formed a very clear boundary that differentiated us from others. This was a totally new environment for us.

The experience of coming into the physical gave birth to beliefs in lack and limitation, which in turn gave birth to wars and disputes over resources, and the belief that we need to control and manipulate our environment and everyone in it. Essentially, all of these things were born out of fear. As we look at the evolution of humanity, we see a steady path of evolution from being purely in survival mode, meaning that our focus was solely on feeding and breeding, to later believing that in order to survive we needed to challenge and vanquish our neighbours (the great empires are testimony to this), and in recent generations we have begun to see the importance of interpersonal relationships and co-operation.

How does all this fit in with great-grandmother's original experience? As humanity perceived lack, it manifested wars and tribal conflicts and the belief that to have power we needed to control others. As these beliefs were put into action, trauma was created and, along with it, dominant thoughts and beliefs concerning the precariousness of life were given birth to. There has barely been a generation since the dawn of time when war has not tarnished and touched us. In generations gone by, the world was not only believed to be an unsafe place; plenty of evidence of that was manifest. With these dominant beliefs, more experience was drawn. War and trauma were brought into the direct experience of our ancestors, which then gave birth to even more wars and trauma in the generations to follow, and so on and on. If you grow up in a world where there is a great belief in lack and limitation and the belief that the only way to have enough is to resist or control others, then collectively and individually the Law of Attraction brings these very things into your experience. It is not great-grandmother or great-grandfather's fault for having drawn these experiences to themselves, for they, like us, were born into a family system and into the beliefs systems that were prevalent within humanity at the time of their birth, and they too have their own ancestors that passed on feelings, emotions and belief systems to them. War, poverty and disease were all part of the accepted norm of reality for them. Just as we would not blame a young child for not understanding calculus, so it is unwise to blame previous generations for the limiting beliefs and limited expectations we have inherited from them. In fact, as we look at the world today, there has been a gradual shift over many generations towards wealth, greater health and co-operation with neighbours, and this shift is gathering speed in many parts of the world. Previous generations were dominated not only by wars, but also by personal family tragedies such as a high rate of infant mortality and death through illnesses that are today easily cured. This has been the work of the previous generations, each one creating a shift in the way in which reality unfolded, through their desires and the evolution of their prevailing thought. When we look at the development of modern medicine that alleviates much family tragedy, we must also acknowledge the role of war in all of that. War has often been the motivator behind the development of the technologies we enjoy today, including surgical and medical procedures. Much experience has been gained on the battlefields. On the macro scale, our great-grandparents were a part of and were influenced by the expectations and beliefs of their generation; on a personal scale, they had experiences that have been transferred to us as individuals.

When we look at history, it is easy to understand why individuals believed such things as "women are not safe", "money does not grow on trees", "when you get old, you get sick", and the myriad of beliefs that so many of us still hold onto today. However, all of the evidence that supports those beliefs was created a long time ago when humanity was crossing the bridge from non-sentience to sentience. I have long thought that the biblical story of Adam and Eve was a description of this journey. As pre-sentient beings, we lived in paradise. When we wanted to eat, our needs were met; when someone died, we accepted that; it was all part of the wheel of life. As the mass of our brains increased, our species developed the capacity for sentience and we became self-aware – in other words, we ate of the Tree of Knowledge of Good and Evil. At that point we became aware of contrast as we observed our world, and the preservation of the body became much more than the preservation of the species: it became the preservation of our awareness of self – in other words, the ego. We began to see that which we sought after and to compare it to that which we did not want. However, as we live in a vibrational universe, it is that very self-awareness and the perception of difference between that which is desired and that which is not wanted, that has led to many things that are not wanted being brought into our experience through the process of prevailing thought. As we emerged from non-sentience into self-awareness instead of readily accepting the fate of death, we began to resist the demise of self and this then became our *modus operandi*. All around us, we began to see threats to our very existence, and the survival of the self became paramount. With survival being the dominant thought, a reality was created in which survival was necessary and the motivator behind all the wars and conflicts, we began not to allow others to be as they are, and we began to control others and our environment. As our paradise was lost and the dominant thought of survival took its grip on humanity, the world we lived in began to be formed according to predominant thought. No longer was there a world of plenty; there was a world of lack, which in turn manifested in personal and mass events. The impact of this we still live with today, not only in terms of what we see manifest in our world, but also in the beliefs that continue to create much of the evidence we see by virtue of the Law of Attraction for us as individuals and collectively as nations, peoples and races.

The twentieth century saw enormous leaps forward for humanity, although in the early part of the twenty-first century we still see evidence of many problems in the world. The First and Second World Wars of the twentieth century brought large-scale death and destruction to many in the world and, as a result of that, a large portion of humanity unleashed a great desire for a better life, a life of peace and prosperity. Consequently, we have seen huge changes in terms of the relative health and wealth of many in the world today. We perhaps remember stories that our parents or grandparents told of saving up for months to buy a new piece of furniture, or that their annual holiday was a day at the beach, or of even harder times when meat was only eaten once a week, or that shoes were handed down from one child to the next. Although this is still true for many in the world today, and even some within the developed nations of the world, by and large, wealth, along with a plethora of lifestyle choices, is increasing along with life expectancy.

Desire has been the mother of all inventions, for just as humanity can conceive of a solution, so it comes to pass. New technologies are born, new solutions are found, and it all comes down to belief. That which we desire comes to fruition.

What is important to remember is that humanity is on a path of evolution. This evolutionary process is one primarily of consciousness and self-awareness. For some, the world seems to be a far more dangerous place than before, whilst for others it is becoming a place of even more possibilities. When we look at developed nations today, we witness the many problems within society – teenagers and young people in crisis, crime, high rates of divorce, single parent families and an abundance of conditions, such as Attention Deficit Syndrome, that were hitherto undefined. What are we to make of all of this? As previously stated, we are not islands and therefore these issues are not held in isolation but are part of the bigger picture of human trauma. What the parents and grandparents feel as a result of their experience, so too do the children, and it is both my belief and my experience through my work that the youth of today are merely acting out what was unspoken in previous generations. With today's youth, the universal principle of "that which is excluded will be represented (or included)" holds true. What we have seen in previous generations is that the expression of emotion and feelings was highly suppressed. This was in part owing to the societal norms of the day upheld by religion, but it was also a defence mechanism against all the trauma that had been experienced. The only way in which an individual can survive war, multiple infant deaths, loss through disease and oppressive work conditions is to suppress emotion. In this way, previous generations could stuff their feelings away so as not to be conscious of the depth of the pain they were in. However, as each of us is part of a greater family system that spans several generations, when feelings are "stuffed" the family soul becomes like a balloon that is squeezed on one side, causing the other end of it to bulge out. Feelings do not disappear when they are suppressed, they simply resurface elsewhere. This leads grandparents and parents to feel dumbfounded when they look at the younger generations of today who suffer from depression and all manner of psychological and emotional ills. Fortunately, today, rather than being labeled as simpletons or as retarded, many of the young in our society who are suffering have a wide variety of assistance available to them. However, it is important to remember that anyone in need is part of a family system, and it is within the system that we can identify both the problem and the solution.

Transformation

So far we have discussed belief systems and their origin and have also revealed how we have hidden loyalties that limit our ability to make any great changes in our lives. In the previous chapter on hidden loyalties, the tools I have shared with you for identifying hidden loyalties and their origins will go a long way to release you from feelings of guilt towards others who have suffered. What more can you do? The answer is, become aware of your thinking.

Much of our thinking is habitual and repetitive; we repeat the same images in our mind over and over and over again. In my book The Language of the Soul, I placed great emphasis on realizing simple truths in order to break our habitual thoughts that create perceptions that are often far from the truth. The habitual thoughts – for example, "my mother doesn't love me" – create prisons from which we view and interpret the world. When we take the time to analyze and delve into our thought patterns and beliefs, we soon begin to realize that much of what we do believe is based on perception or has been taken on from another person. When we become aware of the circumstances and events that impacted our ancestors, it becomes much simpler to identify where our beliefs came from. Add to that an appreciation and understanding of hidden loyalties and how to release them, and we can then continue with the work of transforming our beliefs into those that are more supportive of who we wish to become and how we want to experience our lives.

CHAPTER FIVE

DISCOVERING ESSENCE

It is important that we question our actions, beliefs and motivations. Not that we want to become indecisive or paralyzed by so much questioning that we can no longer move forward! Rather, we need to ask ourselves if our motivation or choice to do, be or become something is borne out of our excitement and bliss or is borne out of habitual thought, limiting beliefs, our perception of external expectations, or fear. So often we get tied up in wanting to do the "right thing" that we forget to really listen to our inner impulses.

Many of us have become accustomed to ignoring our own feelings, as we grew up in families and educational systems that did not encourage independent feeling or thought but instead presented us with beliefs, ideas and a set of feelings that were judged to be either appropriate or inappropriate. As children we learnt to suppress our thoughts and feelings for fear of being rejected in some way, and many of us had the experience of being shamed for not conforming to family and societal rules. This taught us that what was inside us was not reliable, could get us into trouble, or was untrustworthy in some way. In this way we learnt to suppress our emotions and feelings and this suppression gives rise to our challenge in discovering the essence of who we are, for our feelings are the gateway to essence. Discovering our essence is about giving ourselves permission to have the freedom to be who we are and divesting ourselves of the masks we have adopted. Negative emotion is the antithesis of freedom, for we cannot be free when we are burdened with feelings of shame or guilt about who we truly are.

When we consider living a soul-driven life, many questions and issues arise. So many of us fall into the trap of believing that somehow our mission in life is simply to discover the purpose our own soul has for us and, if only we could find that secret to ourselves, life would be much clearer and less complicated. However, the notion that our life's purpose is some divinely-given mission that, once we find out what it is, would make us happy, is rather limiting in its scope. When we consider fate and the world being as it is, then clearly the notion that we are perhaps here to save the world, save others, or undertake a sacred divine mission simply does not fit in with that view of the world. Our mission, if we insist on calling it that, is simply what we ourselves wish it to be. We are not in service to a greater, more powerful omnipotent being, but to ourselves. We have not come to this physical existence in order to prove ourselves worthy of some other more "holy" place, but to seek growth through experience, and our experiences are of our own making and choice, even when we don't believe that they are. One of the reasons so many are locked into the notion that life's purpose is some divinely-held secret that we must discover, is that we have been taught from a very young age that which is good, that which is bad, and that which is the better, more logical and right thing to do. What we have done is to transpose the feelings of wanting to do what pleases our parents onto trying to figure out what the universe wants us to do. This notion is also supported by religion that presents us with a list of the right and correct things to do, believe and feel. Not that all of religion's rules and guidelines are a bad thing, for certainly the Ten Commandments and other similar teachings are a good basis for harmonious living. What is important to remember is that it is the trying to "figure out" what is right or wrong for us that is at the heart of the problem when we want to uncover our life's purpose or essence, for it is our world of feelings that holds the key to all of that.

When we begin to embrace the simplicity of truth and the simplicity of ordinary love, and have surrendered all of the stories and scripts that only seek to limit our lives, we are then open to simple gratitude: gratitude for life, abundance and all the things and people around us that bless our lives on a daily basis. As we open to gratitude, we become more aware of what feels good for us and our searching takes on a different meaning. When we are searching for life's purpose, it is born out of a yearning, and yearning only exists when we perceive a lack of the thing we are searching for. As we embrace simplicity, those things that once seemed to elude us become visible under our very noses, and the yearning lessens and eventually ceases to be, for we are no longer looking for the thing that has been with us all along. When we reach that place, we can then simply ask ourselves, "What would I like to do now, what would I enjoy?" Our life's purpose or mission is whatever we want it to be, whatever feels good for us to do in the moment. There is no great secret to this; it is whatever fulfills you. As simplicity increasingly becomes a part of our day-to-day view of the world, we are in a much better position to become aware of our own true essence. Our own true essence is not some spiritual concept of what we believe "soul" to be, but it is the core of who we are, what makes us tick. What makes us "tick" is the same thing that makes us feel good, excited, enthusiastic and energized.

Not All Created Equal

Wouldn't the world be a tiresome place if we were all the same? If all souls were the same, we would all surely be striving towards the same thing. Whilst it is true that the soul on all levels seeks to be inclusive, it is not true to say that all souls express themselves in the same way. Some of us want to be bakers, others architects, still others accountants, and yet others want to be the best parent they can possibly be. Discovering our life's purpose is no more mysterious than asking ourselves what we love doing; it really doesn't get more complicated than that. However, many of us get bogged down in trying to imagine how it is that we would be able to sustain ourselves financially if we went off and simply did what we love to do. When we look at those who have become rich and famous, especially those that started their lives at the opposite end of the wealth scale, it is clear to see that each of them has made their fortune by doing exactly what they wanted to do and not giving up on their dreams. When we simplify our lives and leave our stories where they are, we can get a much clearer picture. Whilst we are still bogged down with the stories of "my mother didn't love me" or "my brother was the favourite child" or any other stories we have built up over years, our life, our hearts and our minds are full of clutter. With all that clutter we cannot get a clear picture of who we are or even what we want to do! It is all the clutter that makes the task of discovering and living our life's purpose so difficult and elusive.

So what is it that you want to do? How do you wish to express yourself? It is very important that before you choose how you wish to express yourself you first get a sense of what it is that you wish to express. Are you:

Creative? A motivator? An organizer? Artistically expressive? Adept at re-structuring? Good at seeing the big picture? Empathetic? Practical? Precise? Entrepreneurial?

What is the essence of you that makes you feel good when you are expressing it? By that I do not mean what makes you feel good because others feel good when you are expressing it, but what makes *you* feel good because you are expressing the better part of yourself and in those moments you feel more deeply connected to something that is greater than yourself – and yet is you, the true you.

Let me take you into my own personal process with this. When I first started working with others I knew that I loved to communicate with others, be that in writing or talking. As time went by, I became more specific: I love to communicate truth. However, that was still a "doing" or action statement. With a little courage I meditated further and realized that the times when I felt the best when communicating truth were those precious moments when I felt totally connected to Source in a timeless space. I realized that in those moments I had become "the presence of truth" and that this was the essence I was striving to live on a day-to-day basis. Whenever these moments touched me it felt as though time had stood still and the words I was speaking simply fell out of thin air with no thinking process at all; words of truth were simply spoken. Being "the presence of truth" was not about speaking truth to others; it was more about being the presence of my own truth, without masks, pretenses and distortions. Of course, as we live our own true self, others benefit from that as a sort of by- product, and that is also a wonderful thing.

As I relate this feeling to you I am reminded of a public talk I gave about two years ago. I arrived at the venue and only knew vaguely what I would speak about on that particular evening. I had decided that it was far better to get a sense of the audience first, then to speak about what felt appropriate. I greeted everyone and began to speak on the topic of healing. After a couple of minutes, that special feeling came, a feeling of being inspired and truly connected to my audience. I felt alive and glowing from the inside out. After a while I decided to take a break and said to the audience, "Well, I'm sure I've been talking for about forty-five minutes, so let's have a tea break". As I said that, I noticed the silence in the room and looked at the faces. Several had tears rolling down their faces, many were clearly moved. I wondered what had I said. It all felt so good to me. A moment later, the host of the venue came up to me and said, "That was beautiful, but you've been talking for two hours, not forty-five minutes".

The point of sharing this story is to encourage you to ask yourself what feels blissful and timeless to you when you do it. What gives you a great feeling of satisfaction? When we are connected to essence we are far less concerned about what others are thinking and more concerned about how we feel when we are connected. The greatest gift we can give to others is to be connected to our own essence; as a by-product of our own bliss or connectedness, they, too, can benefit. It is clear to all of us that we savour and enjoy much more being in the presence of one who loves what they are doing, than being in the presence of one who is doing what they are doing because they do not see or believe in other possibilities for themselves.

The other hurdle to uncovering and getting in touch with our life's purpose is the concept that one task or expression is in some way better than, more spiritual than, or more politically correct than another. There are many who believe that their life's purpose must be to help others in a very direct way through becoming healers, therapists or helpers in some way. If that were true, who would then grow the food we eat, design and create the shoes on our feet, build our roads, hospitals and schools? Who would publish and print the books we read or bake the bread we eat or mend the engine of our vehicle when it needs to be tended to? There are people out there who are in their bliss when they bake bread or tinker with a car engine; furthermore, we love to be their customers because it feels good to be in their presence! And so it is with all of us. Stop trying to figure out what is right or the best thing to do and simply do what feels good to do, for when you do that and are truly in your essence, those that you serve do not come to buy your bread or architectural plans or accounts ledgers; they come to you! They come to bathe in the light of your joy, expertise, passion, enthusiasm and know-how.

The key to discovering your life's purpose is to identify those activities that take you into that timeless zone. It is the feeling of only having been doing the thing you love to do for minutes, when in actual fact much time has passed. It is the thing that makes you want to get up in the morning, the thing that you constantly dream of and fantasize about. It is the authentic you in action.

Exercise

Get a piece of paper and start by listing all the things that you love to do, no matter what they are. Do not give any thought as to whether you believe that you can make money doing it, just focus on what makes you feel good.

Then underline all of those things you have identified on your list that seem more joyful than other things that are on your list – perhaps there are just one or two or three. Then write those things you have underlined on a separate piece of paper. Once you've done this, ask yourself what the common thread is between these two or three activities. At first it may not appear obvious.

*Let me give you an example. Whenever I did this list for myself, travel was always at the top of the list. I knew that I did not want to be a flight attendant or a ship's steward or work for a travel agency, so that had me a little stumped for a while. Then I decided to ask myself **why** I love travel. What I discovered was something quite different. I loved to travel because travel was akin to exploration – exploring and experiencing different cultures, landscapes, languages; expanding my horizons, knowledge,*

Exercise, continued

*understanding of the world and the people in it – so in writing
"travel" at the top of my list, what I really meant was exploration!
The second thing on my list was always "teaching/public
speaking". So clearly I wanted to travel and to teach. Well, that
was a great goal and I set my focus upon that. It then dawned on
me that travel was the gathering of information and that
teaching/public speaking was the dissemination of information.
The two activities fit together like a hand in a glove! Travel has
given me wonderful opportunities to observe humanity from
many different perspectives and to see universal truths regarding
humans that perhaps were obscured somewhat behind the veils
and filters of cultures, religions and races. All of this has served me
well in my work.*

*When you see two things that seem unconnected, do not look at the
activity itself, but at what the activity gives you or how you express
yourself within that activity. For me, travel and teaching are
indelibly connected to my desire to be a presence of
communicating truth.*

The Four Principles of Creation

Some time ago I learnt about the Four Principles of Creation. The
principles were communicated to me as the essence of human life
and natural desire.

Love – The complete and total acceptance of what is – in other
words, allowing. Allowing the world to be as it is, allowing others
to be as they are, and allowing ourselves to be who we are. Without
love, there is no free will. When we try to control others, that is not
love.

Health and Well-being – We have become aware that the physical
body has a great capacity to heal itself, for health is our natural state
of being. What we have discovered is that hidden loyalties and
entanglements in the fate of others lead us to cut off our natural
state of health, as does our habitual thinking. Well-being is

expressed in all areas of our lives, not only the physical body. We can experience relationship well-being, financial well-being, emotional well-being and mental well-being.

Abundance – The unifying field of consciousness that we have come to know as God or, as quantum physics names it, the Zero Point Field, is a field of infinite possibilities. The universe does not know lack and limitation, for lack and limitation only exist in the mind of humanity.

Creativity – Quantum physics is showing us that the world, the universe and everything in it come into existence as the result of the observer. The observer implies the need for consciousness and awareness; therefore it is our very thinking that creates the world as it. We have the power within us to create reality as we wish to experience it – perhaps with more love, better health, more well-being and more abundance.

You, the Creator

As we have already discussed, it is no coincidence that many members of one family of many generations can experience the same circumstances, even though the circumstances may seem unrelated in terms of the generation in which they occurred. What we have seen is that there are two main ingredients that create repetitive disruptive life patterns: hidden loyalties and inherited belief systems. If our grandfather went bankrupt, we may be predisposed to financial difficulties either as a result of inherited belief systems concerning money, or out of loyalty to his suffering. If our ancestors were slaves, we may be predisposed to living a life that feels like struggle and slavery for the same reasons. If our ancestors were perpetrators that mistreated others, we may feel unknowingly compelled to pay a kind of "penance" for the wrongdoing of others. However, we do not need to be subject to these limiting ancestral patterns. The key to releasing such patterns is to acknowledge and respect the fate of others, get clear about what belongs to us and what belongs to another – in other words, disentangle ourselves from that which is not our business but the business of another.

If you have accepted the notion that we create our own reality and yet have had difficulties in creating life as you want it to be, now is the time for you to re-visit the chapter on Hidden Loyalties. However, there is another important element to discuss here, the natural hierarchy of creative flow. Grandparents give the gift of life to parents and parents pass on the gift of life to children. The body is not just an animated machine; it has life force, and that life force is the same as the pure creative energy that emanates from the Unifying Field of Consciousness. This life force energy is passed down through the generations, each generation passing on not only life but the evolution of awareness, desires, expectations and consciousness down through the many generations. If we go back far enough, back through the mists of time to our far distant ancestors, and then a little beyond that, there exists only the creative Unifying Field of Consciousness. This creative life force energy, whilst we are in physical form, passes to us via our ancestors; in other words, the previous generations act as a conduit through which this energy can reach us. In essence, it is our ancestors who create the opportunity for us to tap into this energy whilst we are in physical form. Now imagine for a moment that your parents are standing behind you, and that their parents stand behind them, and behind your grandparents stand your great-grandparents, and so on. You will begin to see that there is a vast flat triangle fanning out behind you.

The flow of this creative life force energy is hierarchal in nature; in others words, it travels through the preceding generations before it reaches us, and we are placed at the receiving edge of that hierarchy, the tip of the triangle. So it stands to reason that if we are not at the tip of the triangle, we are not in the best place to receive that energy. How does it happen that we can be in the wrong place? This creative energy is passed from grandparents to parents and then to us, but if we do not receive our parents fully, we are unable to receive the natural flow. But wait a moment, aren't I an eternal soul and don't I possess my own source of creative life force energy? Yes, that is true. However, at this moment in time you are focused in physical reality and this experience of physical reality has only been made possible by those who gave you the opportunity to be in physical life, your parents. Therefore, when a child (at any

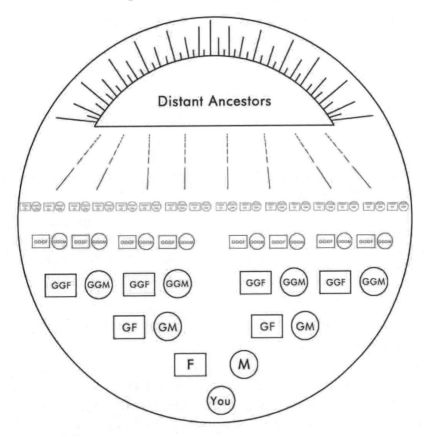

Distant Ancestors

GGGF: Greatgreat Greatgrandfather   GGF: Great Grandfather
GGGM: Greatgreat Grandmother   GGM: Great Grandmother
GF: Grandfather GM: Grandmother F: Father M: Mother
CH: Child

age) places himself or herself above a parent, the child is no longer at the receiving point of creative life force energy. It is not that you are cut off, but you will have placed yourself in a tributary of the flow instead of being in the main channel. In this tributary you may have created financial wealth for yourself, but you will lack something elsewhere in your life, perhaps a loving relationship. You may have created great health, but you may lack wealth, and so on. The best place to be is in the main channel of flow. We do that by honouring fully those who have given us the opportunity to be here in this physical life, no matter how they were as parents. Life in itself is a great gift, the greatest gift that can ever be given.

How do we end up in the tributary?

We end up in the tributary whenever we decide that we could have had better parents or that the ones we have are simply not good enough.

Marci

Marci reported that one area in her life that was not working for her was relationships. She seemed unable to attract a man with whom she could have a loving relationship. I asked her about her family and this is what she had to say:

"My parents have a very rocky marriage and my mother has put up with a lot of abuse over the years. I find it so difficult to have any respect for her – in fact, I really don't respect her that much at all".

I replied to her, "So do you feel that you are a better woman than your own mother?"

"Yes", she replied. "I would never put up with that kind of behaviour. I've made choices in my life".

After this brief conversation with Marci I pointed out a couple of things to her. The first was that her parent's marriage and choices were really none of her business and that she in no way could ever really know the absolute truth of their relationship. The second was that she could not possibly be a better woman than her mother, as it was her mother who gave her life, and therefore all of her "better" qualities simply would not be if it weren't for the gift of life from her mother. I also pointed out that if she could not take her mother fully as her mother then she neither belonged to her female line nor to the world of women and so was not in a good position to attract a man into her life. Marci quickly realized that her entanglement in her parents' affairs and indeed her superiority exacted a very high price: her own loneliness.

Peter

Peter was struggling financially. He reported going from one job to another having great difficulty initiating anything, and experiencing periods of unemployment in between. When I asked him about his family history he reported that his father was an alcoholic, a womanizer and a man that he simply could not respect. I shared with Peter that whilst a woman nurtures life, a man initiates life. He felt deeply ashamed of his father and I encouraged him to consider all of the positive aspects of the man who had indeed initiated his own life. Peter's perception began to change. Once we had done some trans-generational healing work, he got a much clearer picture of how his father was yearning for his own father and expressing that with alcohol. In a poignant and gracious movement, Peter was able to bow to his father and become his son without question.

The point to relating these stories is to demonstrate that when we do not honour the ones who gave us the opportunity to be present in life, we take ourselves out of the main stream of pure, positive, creative life force energy. It does not matter if we look at these scenarios from a spiritual point of view or from a purely human point of view. Spiritual beliefs may tell us that we are in a cycle of reincarnation. If that is true, then surely the parents and the ancestors need to be honoured for having given us the opportunity to incarnate this time around and to work with the patterns we have inherited from them. From a purely human perspective, taking the eternal quality of the soul out of the equation, then our parents gave us life! What greater gift is that? Either way, when we disparage, denigrate or feel ourselves superior to those who gave us life, we take ourselves out of the flow. It cannot be any other way.

Exercise

Imagine for a moment that your parents are standing behind you, and that their parents stand behind them, and behind your grandparents stand your great-grandparents, and then your great-great-grandparents, and so on. You will begin to see the vast, flat triangle fanning out behind you. In your mind's eye, see this stretching back as far as your imagination can take it and begin to see all of your ancestors emerging. Some will be from different cultures, different races perhaps, from different periods of time and perhaps from different parts of the planet. Perhaps you will see Viking warriors, Roman soldiers, African hunters and chieftains, farmers, priests, horsemen, warrior women and also

---

Exercise, continued

those closer to you. Now take this image in your mind's eye even further back, and then even further back, and you'll notice that it becomes a little misty, but in that mist there will be a light, the spark of life force energy that started it all. Now imagine that you are turning to look directly at your parents. As you do so, glance over their shoulders at the vast crowd of ancestors. Look up and down the many generations standing before you and get a sense of their experiences, their dreams, their hopes, their knowledge, their triumphs and how they overcame suffering, wars and challenges in order to pass on life to the next generation. Take a moment to let this all sink in. In front of you is the vastness of human evolution of body, mind and spirit – a veritable treasure chest of gifts that have been handed to you. Now look at your parents and grandparents more directly, knowing that all of this has been passed down to you by them, for they made it possible for you to be here. Inwardly bow to them, knowing in your heart that you cannot stand above any of them, for it is simply impossible. Feel the gratitude well up in your heart.

This inner movement will ensure that you are in the main flow of creative life force energy, the same energy that created worlds, solar systems and indeed the entire universe.

When we are in the main flow, not only are we able to create the life that we want and bring about a more complete expression of the Four Principles of Creation; we also have a much deeper sense of belonging and of who we are.

This meditation is available from www.fourprinciples.com under the title "Healing Relationships".

Accepting Fate

Quite often when I use the term "accepting fate" or "submitting to fate" with groups or individuals, it brings up a lot of resistance, for most people interpret accepting fate as meaning accepting uncomfortable or painful conditions. What I mean by this, however, is the ability to accept the conditions that were given to you at birth and during your formative years. When we resist our fate, we resist what is, and what is cannot be changed. The only thing that can be changed is how you feel about your fate and *what you choose to do with your fate.* Resisting what is only brings more of the same. Many of us spend so much time thinking about where we've been, that we give little attention to where we want to go. When our attention is placed mostly in where we have been, we remain in the same place, not much changes and the past becomes a burden instead of transforming into our companion and teacher. Submitting to fate is about accepting the lot you were given at the start of your life. It is about choosing to use your given fate as a springboard to greater things.

Once we have fully submitted to fate, fate transforms into destiny.

So let us talk about fate. What is it? Fate is, simply, the given facts of your life. You were born male, female or trans-gendered; you were born Caucasian, Asian, African, European, as an American, a Canadian, a Native American or Russian; you are either short or tall, thin or rotund, have straight or curly hair, have an appearance that is considered beautiful or plain, and your feet are a certain size. Well, that is part of it, but there is much more. You were also born into a long line of ancestors and to parents. Your parents may have been abusive, nagging, alcoholic, perhaps they even gave you up for adoption, or your family died in the Holocaust or perhaps deep wounds exist owing to the American Civil War, the Russian pogroms, starvation, tragic accidents – to name but a few possibilities. Perhaps your mother died when you were eight years old, or your father left the family home and you never saw him again and you lost out on education as your mother struggled to make ends meet on her own. All of these things are your fate, as well. They cannot be changed but are, so to speak, a "done deal". When we bemoan the past and justify our lacks in the present, we create more lack in the future. However, fate can be your greatest friend and ally, for within your fate lies your greatest strength.

A difficult fate gives birth to desire, for it places a focus upon the contrast of where you want to be versus where you have been. As we live in a world of opposites – hot and cold, up and down, want and not want, love and hate, freedom and repression, etc. – fate can be used as your springboard from "worse" into that you which is greater than who you are today. In this world of opposites and contrast, you were perhaps exposed to much of what you did not want in earlier years. However, these very circumstances can be turned to your advantage as you consider the flip side of every condition and focus upon the positive aspects. For example, if you grew up in poverty, you understand that all the money in the world does not change the essence of who you are, only how you express yourself. Therefore the poverty in itself can be your ally, friend and guide through life as you move towards more prosperity. When you say to yourself, "I was born into poverty and therefore I have been denied this and that", your focus remains on the poverty. If, however, you say, "I was born into poverty and it taught me the value of both myself and others", you are then using your poverty as a springboard into greater abundance.

I have worked with many individuals who make statements such as, "My parents had a very unhappy marriage; they should never have been married", and then wonder why their lives are not working for them. They don't yet realize that that very statement is the nullifying of their own existence, for had their parents not married, their child would probably not even be here.

Regarding fate, we need to ask ourselves what it is that we are going to do with it, for fate does not go away; it is a given; it won't change, no matter how much you resist it. Many of us fall into the trap of thinking that if we resist our given fate we will change the circumstances of our lives, but the opposite is true. The more we resist it, the more things remain exactly the same. When we acknowledge – indeed, embrace – our fate, and view it as a gift from which we can learn and grow, we flourish.

Fate is much larger than the individual. It is a force that can be felt but not resisted. Let me give you an example.

If I stand on high and look at the colonial powers of Europe and exclaim, "That is a bad thing, it should never have happened", and also have the power to eradicate that history, I would disappear into thin air in the blink of an eye. I am of mixed heritage, my father being English, my mother (late) being Gibraltarian. As Gibraltar is a British colony, then my life, in this form, in this body, simply would not be, had the English not colonized a good portion of the world. Likewise, if you are an African-American or a Jewish American, who and where would you be had it not been for slavery or the holocaust? Sometimes these concepts are a little hard to swallow, for it sounds as if we are approving of or condoning such atrocities. This is not what is being said. What I want you to understand is that fate, being a force greater than yourself, has dealt you a life that you may otherwise not have – in fact, had those histories not occurred, then you simply would not be you as you know yourself today.

Submitting to fate is also a movement of deep inner respect for all that has passed before. In essence, it is a movement of gratitude towards those who survived that suffering in order to pass on life to you, and a movement of gratitude towards the fate itself that brought you to this time and place. When we are in the presence of the soul, we inherently understand that there is a far bigger picture than we can grasp in any one moment, and we have an innate understanding of the sacredness of all life, no matter how it came about. Just as war can be the "father of peace", war can also be the "mother" of the next generation. The generations that follow such events give birth to new desires and new ways of thinking, doing and being.

Fate is our companion though life; we can either befriend it or resist it. We have a choice, and that choosing has consequences which are either more of the same, or something greater, more expanded and magical. When we submit to fate we exhale and the souls of our ancestors exhale along with us, for the soul understands that that which has been excluded will be included. Exclude your fate and you will include the circumstances of the past in your present and in your future. Include your fate and accept what is, and as you exhale you will give birth to a whole new world.

Peace begins with the presence of the soul, and the essence of the soul is acceptance and allowing – in other words, love. The soul does not resist, it does not try to conquer or vanquish, it neither laments nor bemoans, neither seeks vengeance nor offers itself up as martyr. The soul acknowledges and accepts what is. The path to discovering your essence is the path of least resistance to what is, for as we resist what is, we are in direct contrast to the nature of the soul; but as we accept what is, as we exhale, we bring the soul closer, and as we do this we can experience a greater portion of who we truly are and shift our focus towards our aspirations and desires, for that which we focus upon comes to be.

You may be thinking that you have been in touch with your desires and yet all the things that you desire have not materialized. It is important to understand the difference between desire and longing or yearning. Longing and yearning only exist as emotions when we are focused on the lack of what we want or on how things were. It is only out of desire that is focused on where we want to be, that the focus of our desire can come to be.

We naturally desire to have and live a life that expresses the Four Principles of Creation, for that is the universal nature of things – indeed, the nature of the soul. We naturally desire well-being, better health, more abundance, love, the ability to accept, and our innate power to create what we want with our lives. Our fate may have given us great lack in one or more of these areas; however, what fate has done is to hand us a tool with which we can launch ourselves towards that which we naturally desire.

CHAPTER SIX

EXPERIENCING THE PRESENCE
OF THE SOUL

When we experience the presence of our own soul, we live on the throne of peace. I use the word throne, for when we are in contact with our inner being, the soul, we know and understand that we are the king or queen of our kingdom, that we create our own reality, that we are responsible for our reactions and responses. We live our truth without hesitation. The soul understands that it is creator and that it stands in a place of allowing and accepting that which others create, knowing that it cannot be affected by others unless it lends its attention to them.

When we experience and live the presence of our soul, we also understand the following:

- That there is much more to us than our five senses
- That we are eternal beings with no ending and no beginning
- That we are connected to all life
- That it is not only our deeds that contribute to the world, but also our thoughts and our energy.

Indications that we are living with the presence of our soul include:

- A sense of peace. We understand and know that all is well in the world and all is exactly as it should be.
- Acceptance and allowing. We understand that in the grand scheme of things everyone on earth today will at some stage also consciously experience the presence of their own soul and that, in accordance with the free will present in the universe, others are simply creating their experience. We also

understand that we cannot change others, not matter how hard we try, and we surrender the need to convince others of our way of thinking, being or doing.

- Truth. We begin to live a life devoid of stories and drama, and we begin to focus on the simplicity of truth, the simplicity of love, and the simplicity of gratitude. We no longer feel the need to ingratiate ourselves with others or to seek their approval. We feel secure in our own truth and are at peace with the many truths that others hold.

- Abundance. We begin to understand that abundance is our natural birthright in all areas of our lives, for as souls we are connected to the infinite creative forces of the universe.

- Well-being. We are no longer vexed by the ills in the world and we have a deeper understanding that all is well, not only with the planet, but with every person, including ourselves. We understand that well-being is the natural state of the creative life force energy of the universe and that we may tap into that at will, at any time.

Many are now increasingly beginning to understand and to experience that which is beyond the five senses. Although we have lived in an age where, for the most part, science has denied the existence of anything outside of our five senses and anything that cannot be measured, we are beginning to see a merging of some sections of science with the ancient teachings of some spiritual traditions – for example, physics and metaphysics are coming together to form new sciences. Hitherto our culture has venerated the intellect above all else, but now, gradually, we are beginning to see and experience the value of the world of our feelings and of the subtle energies that surround us. Many more of us are becoming accustomed to placing value on our intuition and our "gut feel". As we live the presence of our soul, we become much more in tune with the more subtle energies around us and we begin to respond less to what is logical and more to what feels right. Until recent decades, the world of intuitive insights, pre-cognition and direct experience of that which is outside of our usual perception field of the five senses rested solely in the realm of mystics and psychics. Today, however, more and more people are becoming aware of how much more there is to the world than can be seen, and there is increasing experience and acceptance of what we can feel.

About a decade ago I went on a Zen retreat for four days. At the outset I found it grueling and wondered why I had allowed myself to be talked into this arduous setting. I wondered why I was there, what was the point and would I get anything out of this experience at all, aside from a sore bum as a result of sitting in virtually one spot for almost eighteen hours a day. On the third day, I was sitting opposite an older woman, looking at her intently. The more I looked, the more different she looked, and then I began to notice that she had a subtle glow about her. I then noticed that the glow was much more than that: it had substance, and indeed movement. Suddenly, I could not see the woman at all; what I saw was a vibrating and pulsating energy field. She had become transparent and I could see straight through the space where her physical body would have been, right to the wall behind her. I then noticed that the wall itself was glowing and indeed had movement, and I changed my focus from the woman in front of me to the wall behind her, for I was totally spellbound and intrigued by my experience. As I gazed at the wall, it, too, became translucent and I began to see in great detail the courtyard of the monastery in which I was staying. I was astounded; I was looking straight through a wall! The experience then became significantly more intense and everything and everyone simply became energy. From my point of view, I was swimming in a sea of light. As the light became more intense, a feeling came over me that I had never experienced before: it was if I was everywhere. I had no awareness of my body at that stage, and no awareness of where I stopped and other things started. In this state of consciousness I was the older woman, the wall, the courtyard, the furniture, the ceiling, the floor, and everyone and everything else, whilst still retaining an awareness of being me. The experience was beyond words and not in the least bit frightening; I had never felt so safe in all of my life. It was as if all of my inhibitions had floated away. There was nothing to be afraid of and no doubt.

Whilst I was in that state of consciousness, images began to flash before me – images of wars, famine, weddings, the smile of a child, images of saints and of those who cause harm to others – many images flashing before me as if on a screen. None of the images, no matter how gruesome, frightened me, or even touched or moved me in any way. I was simply observing them as if from a great distance, not in the least involved. A pivotal moment came as I had the thought, "They are all the same, there is no difference". The moment I had the thought, I felt another rush of energy move through me and it felt as if I was in the centre of the universe, holding all that I could see in my mind as an image. The only thing that was real was me, and all of the things I could see from afar were only images; they were not real. I was fortunate to have a very astute Zen teacher who could see what was happening with me in that moment. He very gently placed a hand on my shoulder and whispered in my ear, "What does it feel like?" Had he not done that, I would have never been able to give this experience words that made sense of it. My reply to him was, It is like being wrapped in a blanket of love, but not just wrapped in it, I am the blanket of love, but being wrapped by it at the same time. I was everything and nothing.

This was my first definitive experience of soul and it has remained with me to this day. What I felt and experienced on that day was that there was no difference at all, from the soul's perspective, between good and evil, between good experiences and bad ones, between good people and bad people; it was all simply experience and all was equal in the eyes of my soul. I remained close to that state of awareness for several hours that day and, as I later walked in the gardens of the monastery, I became increasingly aware of the energies and consciousness of plants, trees and flowers. I stopped for what seemed like an eternity by a rose bush and gazed upon a beautiful pink rose. I felt the rose reach out to me, as if to say hello, and I instinctively said hello back, with a broad smile on my face. Then the most amazing thing happened: I felt myself being drawn into the rose. My entire being was filled with its fragrance. I and the essence of that which is a rose had become one. Without giving a moment's thought as to whether it was silly or not, I asked the rose a question and was astounded and deeply touched by the answer. I had asked the rose, "What is your purpose, why do you exist?" The rose replied, "I am here to remind all of you who have forgotten what beautiful beings you are. We flowers are the healers of humanity, we uplift you through reminding you of beauty, and our fragrance gives peace to the mind so that our message can be heard".

On that day, a woman had become energy in my eyes, I had seen through walls, had seen good and evil as the same, the universe as an image rather than anything real, and had had a conversation with a rose. It was a pivotal experience that would forever change the way I looked at the world and an experience that I would draw upon when I got caught up in all of the illusions of my day-to-day thinking. This had been my greatest debut into the presence of my own soul. The dominant feelings of that entire experience had been total acceptance of what is, an intensity of love that words cannot describe adequately, a sense of being one with and connected to everything and everyone, and a vast feeling of gratitude. Not gratitude for the experience itself, which naturally I do feel, but a vast feeling of gratitude whilst in the experience of feeling my own soul's feelings. My soul was grateful for all experience; it lived an existence that was dominated by gratitude – for everything. Not one thing, not one little morsel of substance, was overlooked, neglected, ignored or went unacknowledged in the heart and mind of my soul. My soul included everything, embraced everything, accepted everything and looked upon everything with a depth of gratitude I had never experienced before. It was truly unconditional love.

Such profound experiences do not come to all of us, and for those of us who have experienced them, they are not everyday experiences. However, what I took away with me from that experience is the constant reminder that the path to inner peace and to our soul is through gratitude and acceptance. As we practice gratitude and acceptance in our day-to-day lives, we open doorways to the greater awareness of our souls and to the infinite.

This experience was just the beginning of my journey into the mystical world of the soul. I hesitate to use the word mystical, for once you have experienced it, that which was labeled mystical seems much more usual. During a similar type of experience, when I found myself traveling out of my body, I could clearly see myself lying in my bed and found it rather odd. I stood at the foot of the bed feeling very curious about the person that was fast asleep and a little perplexed at the need for a body. This feeling passed in a fleeting moment and I found myself floating above the streets and roads of Rotterdam, where I was living at the time. I gazed up at the stars and wondered if I could go to them now that I was out of my body. In the next instant I found myself floating in space right in front of the sun. I just hovered there and stared at it. I was still thinking like the normal me and wondered why it was not hurting my eyes looking directly at the sun, and why it did not feel hot as I was so very close to it. As I was having these thoughts, I became aware that I was not just looking at a fiery ball of gas; the sun was a being, it had awareness, it had consciousness, it was alive. I was awestruck and in my mind I gingerly asked if I could know more about it – I asked gingerly for I had a sense that I was in the presence of a being that was far, far greater than myself. I began to feel a tugging in my solar plexus area and noticed that I was moving closer to the sun, passing through the layers of the corona, then through the fiery mass, and then I entered a whole different world of light – it was vast. As I moved into this new world, deeper and deeper, I saw a huge throne in front of me. Sitting upon that throne was a being of fire and light that to my estimation was the size of the Empire State Building, or larger. I instinctively got down on my knees and bowed and asked, "Are you God?" The response I got was a surprise: my question was met with gentle, friendly laughing. I got up and looked at the being and asked, "Who are you?" I was told that this being represented the collective consciousness of all of the souls of humanity and all that lived in our world. I was told that God was far greater than itself, although they were one. This being then went on to explain to me that the Egyptians and others who had worshipped the sun were not entirely wrong in their beliefs concerning the sun, as many of their mystics had also made the same journey that I had, but had misinterpreted the actual meaning. The Sun Being explained to me that, just as the physical sun sustained life on planet earth, the spiritual sun (this one being one of many) sustained the spiritual energies of all life on earth. Rather than being an individual entity, it was an expression of all souls, human, animal, mineral and plant life on earth and, indeed, in the entire solar system. As I understood these things, I found myself once more standing at the foot of my bed and a moment later I was back in my body and I woke up.

What this experience taught me was that everything is alive, including rocks, mountains, the moon, and indeed our sun, each thing having its own purpose, path of evolution and meaning. I came out of this experience knowing that everything in our world was here out of free will and much of it was in service to humanity. I began to look at animals differently, began to see the nobility in their service to humanity and how even the trees were here to serve and support us in our quest for greater experience. My understanding of the gratitude I experienced from my soul deepened.

The two experiences I have related are just a sample of the many experiences I have had of this nature, and they are very real to me. Though sharing the experiences with you, I wish to communicate that you can open up these doorways to the greater you, not through taking yourself off to a Zen monastery, but through tapping into and practicing the dominant feelings held by the soul – acceptance and gratitude. Even today as I walk through my garden, I regularly thank every tree, plant and flower for their existence, for adorning my world with their beauty and fragrance. I have grown past the stage of worrying whether others think I am crazy for doing this. There have been times when I do question whether my very real experiences were just a result of my imagination or some function of brain chemicals that created a very pleasant experience. Let's say that one or both of those are true. What then? The conclusion that I have come to is that when I do thank my garden for its beauty, it simply feels good to do so, it puts me in a better mood, it makes me feel more positive about life and all of the goodness in the world – so what can be wrong with any of that?

The presence of our soul comes to us when we are quiet and at peace with the world. Many rely on meditation to get into that space. However, whenever we focus on the feeling of gratitude and let the world just be in a state of acceptance, we can become aware of the presence of our soul whilst in living action, not only during meditation.

Exercises

There are many excellent exercises for experiencing the presence of your own soul.

Exercise One

Ensure that you will not be disturbed for about 20 minutes. Take a candle and place it on a table at about eye level when you are sitting in a chair. Sit and gaze into the candle whilst observing your breath. Breathe in through your nose and out through your mouth. If random thoughts come to your mind, simply allow them to dissolve as you place all of your focus on the candle. Within a few short minutes you will feel very relaxed. As you feel this relaxation, place your attention on the area between the eyebrows, also known as the third eye, and imagine that you are looking at the candle through your third eye as well as through your physical eyes. You may feel energy moving in the area of the third eye, or have a sense of something opening. As this happens, begin to look around the room and just note any differences that there may be. Perhaps the colours are more vibrant, or perhaps you simply have the sense of seeing aspects of it that you have never seen before.

Exercise Two

Do the same as above, only this time place a house plant or a flower in a vase close to the candle. After you have engaged your third eye state of awareness, gaze at the plant and imagine that your energy or your thoughts are reaching out to touch the plant. When you are complete with these exercises, jot down your experiences.

Exercise Three

If you do not have a garden, then you may do this exercise just as easily with house plants. Sit or stand in front of a plant and look at it intently. In your mind, or out loud, tell the plant everything you appreciate about it, and tell it in as much detail as you can. Feel your appreciation for the plant and thank it for making your world more beautiful. Then either sit or stand in silence, quiet your mind of thoughts, and simply allow yourself to feel the plant with your other senses. You will be quite amazed at the response you get. You may even receive requests like, "Please move me to that window over there", or, "I need you to water me more frequently in the summer months", or simply a message of, "You're welcome". If you do receive a specific request from the plant, don't dismiss it, for you will find that as you honour the request, the plant will flourish exponentially.

Exercise Four

If you have a household pet, get quiet and enter your meditative space; the pet does not need to be present with you. As you enter that feeling of being more expanded, envisage your pet and begin a dialogue. Tell your pet all the things you appreciate about it and how grateful you are for the sense of security you gain, sense of joy, or whatever feelings the existence of this pet gives you. Once again, when you are complete with sharing your gratitude with your pet, become quiet again and receive anything that your pet may want to share with you. My experience is that cats can be a little more direct than dogs, even abrupt! You'll be amazed at the responses you get from your animals.

I've tried this with the goldfish in my pond, and the experience is rather different; they do not seem to have an emotional field in the same way that domestic dogs, cats and horses do. However, I am very pleased that they feel comfortable enough in their pond to produce offspring and that the offspring live on to become adult fish. Just as with my plants, I let the goldfish know that I am

Exercise Four, continued

grateful for their presence and I thank them for adorning my world with their beauty.

Even when we lead busy lives it is possible, with intention, to take a few moments every day to take in the world around us from the perspective of our soul. The more we practice this, the more it will become second nature. I encourage you to do this even if it feels just plain silly in the beginning. The more we make the choice to see things as our soul does, the more present our soul will be in our day-to-day and moment-by-moment experience in this wondrous world we live in. As we experience the presence of our soul, we will experience increasing levels of peace and find ourselves less and less bothered by what others do.

Other Avenues

We are much more successful at passing through the gateway to the presence of our soul when we are not burdened by negative emotion or the tendency to repress emotion. If you find yourself burdened in this way, there are other avenues you can explore in order to start the process of releasing negative emotion that has been stored in your cellular system and in your energy field. I have experienced the following modalities and ways of working to be very efficient in releasing emotional blockages.

Body Work and Breathwork

The various modalities within this genre that can assist you in releasing emotions that are stored in your physical body include, for example, Rolfing, Postural Integration, Rebirthing, Holotropic Breathwork, Shiatsu, Tai Chi.

Energy Work

Energy work is best performed by those who have been though structured professional training. In my experience, the best energy workers are graduates of the Barbara Brennan School of Healing or the Snow Lion School of Healing. Tai Chi, Chi Gung and the Healing Tao based on the work of Mantak Chia are also excellent pathways.

Therapy Modalities

Family Constellations – an excellent way to unlock yourself from emotions that you are carrying for others, emotions that originate elsewhere in your family. It is also a way to identify trans-generational belief systems and to unlock the original family trauma.

Core Quantum Method – a simple and effective way of unlocking subconscious belief systems.

Several things are very important to consider when choosing to work with any modality that will assist you on your path to greater emotional freedom:

1. Choose to work with a practitioner that you feel comfortable with. It is important to work with an individual who allows you to feel supported in your process whilst at the same time does not enable you in remaining in a place of self-pity or martyrdom.

2. Work with individuals who have sufficient training, experience and know-how in their chosen field of work. I would not recommend that you allow anyone to work on your energy field that has only done a weekend or two of training in Reiki, for example. Although professional training does not guarantee the quality of the person you choose to work with, it is nonetheless a helpful benchmark.

3. Remember that not every modality is for everyone, just as not every therapist is for everyone.

4. Understand the difference between discernment and resistance. If you find yourself not liking most therapists you meet and not liking most modalities you experience, you are probably in resistance.

5. Feeling strong emotion is not the measure of the success of any particular therapy. If feeling strong emotion is new to you, you can become addicted to the process, as it can feel very good to

experience such strong emotion after years of suppression. Some sessions, on the other hand, may be very subtle. Discern the success of any modality by how you are able to integrate the change in the days and weeks after the session, not by how you feel during the session itself. At times, it is the slightest movement that can create great changes in our lives, not the big emotional upheavals.

6. ALWAYS inform any therapist you work with if you have any significant medical conditions, such as high blood pressure, a heart condition, cancer, HIV disease, bi-polar disorder, schizophrenia, other chronic conditions or surgeries.

CHAPTER SEVEN

BECOMING CONSCIOUS
OF WHAT YOU WANT

As we embark upon the path of healing or of creating any change in our lives, we will almost always come to a bridge that needs to be crossed. That bridge asks us: Do you want peace, or do you want to be right?

I laugh inwardly as I ponder this question, for I can imagine that many of you who have just read the question have answered, "Both!", as I have done on many occasions. However, we rarely can have both; it is one or the other. When we declare that we want to heal our lives, we must also become conscious of what we may have to surrender in order to reach our goal of a more complete and fulfilled life. We need to surrender most, if not all, of our stories and a lot of our opinions. Our opinions and stories about others, how things are and how the world is are the greatest prisons that we create for ourselves; they keep us exactly where we are. In order to start releasing our opinions and stories, we must first understand the difference between expressing an opinion and speaking our truth. When we speak our truth, our body relaxes and we are more in contact with our essence. In order for us to become clearer about what we want, we need to practice speaking our truth more, not least to ourselves. Opinions and stories jumble things up, scramble our thoughts and take us into a feeling space that is more removed from the presence of our own soul; speaking our truth brings us closer to our soul.

Becoming conscious of what we want in our lives also means bringing into alignment our thoughts, words and feelings with the object or focus of our desire. When we say, "I need more income but the economy is bad", or, "I want to earn more money, but there's not much call for what I do", we are expressing an opinion that is based on one of our scripts and not on our truth. Or we may say, "I want to feel more joy in my life, but it is difficult knowing that my mother never loved me"; that, too, is an opinion taken from one of our scripts that is not in alignment with truth. Truth always feels good; opinions and stories invariably feel bad.

Many times we say that we want to be more aware of our soul, or attain healing in some area of our lives, but we give it little of our attention. Or, the moment after we have stated our given intention to heal, we start to focus on all the things that are seemingly wrong in our lives, and so we continue to live on the merry-go-round, passing the same old situations and conditions time and time again. Additionally, we spend so much time being reactive to the world that we spend precious little time even considering in any great detail what it is that we want out of life.

In my experience, the vast majority of individuals state what they want from a place of longing or of lack. This is how it goes: "I want more love, but no one loves me", "I want better relationships, but good people are difficult to find", "I want to spend more time getting in touch with who I really am, but I don't know who I am", and so on and so forth. We spend so much time reacting to the world, as opposed to pre-determining our relationship to the world and how we want it to be, that we have very little time to really ask ourselves the most important question of all: What do I want? Also, What am I willing to do or to surrender in order to have what I want? For many, life becomes wasted through being in reactive mode the majority of the time. Time is spent in careers and participating in activities that are based on our fear of lack, and over time we begin to lose ourselves in all of that. Then one day we wake up wondering where we went and what happened to our sense of self, indeed, our essence. When we are reactive most of the time, we incrementally move away from our essence, from the presence of our own soul, until we finally feel that we have no soul at all, or that the way to our essence and soul has been lost – all because we have lost the habit of asking ourselves what we truly want.

Desire versus Longing

Longing exists when we are focused on the lack of that which we want. Desire exists when we have a vision of the possibility of the thing, the relationship, the life condition or the healing becoming present in our lives. Longing feels like a hole in the soul, whereas desire brims with enthusiasm, vision, anticipation, energy, intention, focus and purpose. If as you read these words you are saying to yourself, "I have wanted this or that for most of my life, but nothing has changed", then you are probably dealing with the emotion of longing. If that is so, then you will discover that the majority of your thinking and thought around the subject has been on the lack rather than on the possibility. Most people I have worked with focus mostly on what they do not want and place most of their energy and thinking into wishing to and trying to change others. They want better parents, their spouse or partner to change, or the politics of their country to change; most of it is about the "others", rarely about what they want to change about themselves, their thoughts and their feelings. Many of these people have believed that they cannot change much about themselves until the world and others in their lives also change or, preferably, change first. Very often when I ask a client what they want, they reply with a list of things that they don't want. Thinking about what we want in terms of what we do not want has become a habit for most of us. Changing that habit requires practice. It also requires an ability to take responsibility for our lives and to surrender the need for anyone else to change. Change begins with us, and our experience of reality begins and ends with us. At times, we all want the easy fix, believing that if only "they" would change, then our lives would be much different. However, we've been on this path of wanting others to change for most of our lives, and what has changed? Nothing, or at least not much. When we shift our focus solely to what we want for ourselves, devoid of the need for anyone or anything else to change, then the creative wheels of the universe kick into gear and circumstances begin to change. It is not that the wheels of the universe were not working before; it's that as you focus on the same thing repetitively, the same thing is brought to you over and over again, a little like playing an old record when the needle is stuck.

Practice Makes Perfect

All that is required to change this old pattern of thinking and wanting is practice. If you feel that you have become so reactive to the world that you have lost touch with what you want, then you can start in small ways today to make clear statements about the object of your desire. Journaling is a very powerful way to start the process of focusing your energy onto the things that you want. The more you journal, the more refined and precise the definition of your desires will become and you may be surprised to discover that some of the things you thought you wanted no longer carry any energy of desire for you.

Exercise

Get a piece of paper and write down statements regarding what you want. Write down as many as you can, concerning all areas of your life. Include career, relationships, money, health, home, etc. Once you have your list, re-read them to yourself and underline those that you **really** *want. This will help you to create more focus and to get clear about your true desires. Once you have your list of what you* **really want***, ask yourself if you are really committed to having it. Then ask yourself if anything on your list is dependent on any hidden desire for someone else to change. For example, if you are unhappy about an aspect of your relationship, understand that trying to change the other has never worked and will not ever work. If something on your list is dependent on needing another to change and therefore invokes longing, then redefine what you want in terms of how you wish to experience yourself in the relationship.*

Defining what we really want is a matter of practice. We need to learn how to identify when we are attached to wanting something that we in essence do not really want. I'll give you an example from my own life. I experienced a downward turn in bookings for my workshops and private sessions with clients. I was a little confused and of course stressed owing to the financial implications. I had all of the tools at my disposal and knew exactly how to create what I wanted through visualization, journaling and further defining what I really wanted. I set about visualizing my workshops full, feeling very confident that if I had many repeat clients then the work I did was enjoyed and wanted by others. However, every time I sat in meditation visualizing my workshops in my centre full again, I felt resistance. I could not understand the resistance and decided that the resistance must be linked to a negative belief about my own work, worthiness, etc. I investigated further and discovered that I had healthy confidence levels regarding my work, so that was not the issue. Having decided that I was clear about my skills, ability and sense of pride in my own work, I decided to continue visualizing and to force myself through the feelings of resistance that manifested themselves as my energy dropped during the meditation. I sat in meditation every morning for about three or four days, and again that feeling came. I was so confused and could not understand why this would be happening, for I was sure that this was what I wanted. I then got into fear- based mind chatter, asking myself if this was a "sign" from the universe that I was "supposed" to do something else. I really had to remind myself that the universe only delivers what I want and has no desire that is separate from my own. I pondered some more, and I admit that I worried some more. One morning I simply sat in my chair, not to visualize but to feel my way into what was really going on. Then it hit me and I exclaimed out loud, "I'm so bored!" That was quite a shock. Me, bored with my work? I sat with the feeling of boredom a little longer and allowed it to take over. My next step was to get out my journal and write to determine if I was truly bored with my work. The answer was no, but the feeling was still there. That night I went to bed a worried man; I could hardly believe that I was bored with my work but the feeling was there and I could not deny it. As I fell asleep I asked my soul to reveal to me the nature of my boredom and what it all meant. As I awoke the following morning, the very first thought that came to my mind was, "It's not the work I'm bored with, it's my routine!" What a relief to have this clue. As is my habit, I reached for my journal in order to re-define what it was that I wanted, given that I had now established that it was not the work that was the issue. What became apparent was my desire for more variety, exposure to more cultures, nationalities, ethnicities and locations. As soon as I understood this, I made a clear statement that I now wanted to travel extensively with my work and visit countries that would offer me a great deal of variety. Literally within one week of having gone through this process, an invitation to give a workshop in Scotland was extended to me and, as I write this book, invitations continue to come in from many parts of the world.

The point of sharing this personal story with you is to demonstrate that defining what we want takes both practice and focus. I could have simply given in to worry and allowed circumstances to get worse. However, understanding that the universe delivers to us the subject of our focus, I knew that the only place to find the answer was within me. What I uncovered was that I had been feeling the desire to work in various locations for quite a while but my focus was on my boredom – and that is what manifested, more boredom! Defining what we want is an ongoing, daily refining process.

As we have become primarily reactive beings, my suggestion is that you ease yourself into you new habits with just a little less action and a little more defining of what you want. As time goes by, you'll find yourself reacting far less and creating and drawing to yourself what you really want much more.

Creating Freedom

True happiness comes from creating freedom and from deciding that you will not settle for anything less than being joyful about what you are doing and how you are living your life. If you have created prisons for yourself, it is important that you ask yourself why you are willing to settle for less than what you truly want. When we create these prisons it is because we believe that we don't deserve better, or we have a hidden loyalty somewhere, or simply because our expectations of what we believe is possible for us are limited in some way. Perhaps you were raised with the idea that to have a job, a very secure job, is what is most important. Such beliefs stem from a time when previous generations experienced much lack and scarcity within the backdrop of war and political unrest. When we create such prisons for ourselves, our energy begins to wane and the light of our essence begins to dim.

We also create prisons within friendships and relationships. Perhaps we get caught up in hearing the same woes being told time and time again, and helping the same person over and over again; when we do this, we are in a prison of our own making. Sometimes we worry that to cease listening or to cease helping in some way would make us a bad or unloving person. However, if we are locked in a prison that does not give us joy, eventually there will be no more to give. Freedom cannot exist when there is negative emotion regarding a situation, relationship or friendship. But when we focus on what we want, we release ourselves from bondage and begin to radiate once more. From this place of freedom we are in a far better position to help others, through our example.

Changing the Negative into the Positive

We live in a world that sees most things as being either good or bad. When we turn on the television, listen to the radio or join in conversations, most of the emphasis is on what is bad or wrong with the world. As we have become so accustomed to this negative orientation, we tend to do the same thing when we look at our past. Was it all bad? For many, the past has become a millstone that continues to anchor them in the past, for as we look to the past with negative feeling, we create our present, and indeed our future, based on the same feelings.

I'll give you a typical example of how we become anchored in the past.

Roseanne

Roseanne visited a workshop stating that her life and relationships were not working for her. As we briefly discussed her history she revealed to me that she was divorced and was very angry with her ex-husband. She went on to say how the marriage was terrible and that she had great regrets about ever marrying him. I then went on to ask her if she had ever been in love with her ex-husband, and she replied in the affirmative. She also revealed that, with this man she had once loved, she had brought both a son and a daughter into the world. As part of our work together I assisted her in acknowledging the love that existed between them and the great gift that her ex-husband had given her in the form of her children. As we worked, Roseanne wept and was able to release her anger. She realized that she was focused on her feelings of betrayal and that she was busily creating both her present and her future based upon those feelings. From her one painful experience she had decided that all men were not to be trusted and that all relationships would probably end the same way – and so it came to pass. When we are emotionally anchored to the negative emotion of the past, the past simply re-creates itself again and again.

I return to the statement I made earlier concerning the bridge we will all need to cross whilst on the path of healing: Do we want peace, or do we want to be right? Until our work together, Roseanne wanted to be right. She wanted to be right in her sense that her ex-husband was a scoundrel, a man that betrays others and a lousy partner. In doing this, she swept aside all of the good in the relationship – in other words, all of the wonderful qualities the man had that became the foundation of her love for him, plus the gift of her two children. I asked her to contemplate her ex-husband's positive qualities, all the ones that she had fallen in love with, and I then asked her if she could see some of those qualities reflected in her son and daughter. She again answered in the affirmative and could think of several gifts that her children had received from him in terms of characteristics and personality traits. When we bless the past and see the positive, we are in a much better position to create a present and a future that is more to our liking.

From every negative experience there is always something positive that we have learnt. Perhaps it was courage, determination, self-assuredness, self-awareness or a host of new skills. When you hit rock bottom, the only direction in which to move is upward, and that in itself is a valuable journey. What is important to understand is that one negative experience can and often does lead to the next when we focus upon it. You may be feeling that I am encouraging you to be in denial about what happened. Not at all. However, if your only reference point to the event, experience or relationship is the negative, then that will be your anchoring in the present. We say things like, "This company was bad and my boss was terrible; I hope that the next is not the same", and we then approach a new job with our fears in hand, for it has become our point of reference. Then in the new job similar circumstances prevail and we leave to find yet another. By this time we have two anchor points in negative experience that become our reference point for viewing work and career. As this becomes a more deeply entrenched point of reference, so we continue to re-create the same circumstances with different people again and again until we exclaim that it is an absolute truth about the world and our experience. Have you ever wondered why you continually have "bad luck" whilst others seem to get one "lucky break" after the next? Is it because they are more intelligent, more talented, more attractive? No, it is because they have a reference point regarding an aspect of their life that is different to your own.

When I was in my late teens and very early twenties I had a job which at that point I loathed. I certainly never wanted to do that again and, in my own words, I had "the boss from hell!" As the years have gone by I've begun to look very differently at that job and my function there. Although totally different to what I am doing now, I have come to see it as the first stepping stone to my work with others. The job entailed taking copy over the phone for classified advertisements that would be placed in a national newspaper in the UK. As part of my training, I was taught how to assist others in creating advertisements that were succinct and to the point. This job laid the foundation not only for my books, but also for the way in which I assist clients to clearly define the issue they wish to work with and what it is that they want. Every relationship, every job, every situation has taught us something valuable. We simply need to be willing to look at the gifts and to give up our need to be right or to be vindicated.

When we embark on the path of consciously and deliberately choosing what we want, it is most important that we do not spend time in regretting the past. At times there are things that we do regret – for example, when we become aware that we have hurt others with our words or actions – but that can be easily remedied with a genuine heartfelt apology that is simple, clear and to the point. When we spend time in regret, we are forgetting that we are no longer the same person that did exactly what we knew how to do at that time. When we know differently, we do differently. In other words, we continue to do the same, and therefore get the same results repeatedly, until we learn a different way.

Chapter Eight

GETTING THERE FROM HERE

No matter where you are in your life, once you have begun the process of intentionally and consciously deciding where you want to be, you can get there from here. Every day and every moment has the potential for a new beginning. The only things that ever hold us back are our reference points to the past and how things were. We say things like, "It didn't work out before, I was disappointed then" – and then we often stop in our tracks for fear of experiencing yet another disappointment. It is our fear of pain that often sabotages our success. This strategy is itself an illusion, however, for there is no worse pain than leading a life that doesn't feel like living, or a life not well spent.

To get there from here, you also need to become aware of your life scripts.

> *All the world's a stage,*
> *And all the men and women merely Players:*
> *They have their exits and their entrances;*
> *And one man in his time plays many parts....*

William Shakespeare,
As You Like It, (II, vii, 139–142)

Scripts

As we emerge from childhood into adulthood, we have already formed a script for our life, made up of beliefs and belief systems that we have inherited from our immediate family, from our ancestors and also through observation and experience. These scripts pre-pave our experience of life as they are an expression of what we expect; as we expect, so do we get. As we become a little older and enter into intimate relationships, we add to our script our personal experiences of love, intimacy, men, women, etc. By the time we have reached thirty or thirty-five, our scripts are quite well established; in parts of our lives we are like hamsters on a treadmill, going around in circles, re-creating the same experiences time and time again. It is little wonder that we begin to age after the age of thirty-five; it's exhausting!

Scripts are made up of elements, and these elements are the beliefs we hold true about the world and ourselves. It is often very difficult for us to concede that a belief is simply that, and not an absolute truth, for the world appears to offer support for our belief with seemingly abundant evidence. However, when we take into consideration that we live in a universe based on energy and attraction, and that thought is energy, we understand that the universe will always provide us with copious amounts of evidence to support our belief. If we believe in wealth, it will show us that; if we believe that a supportive and loving relationship is only for the lucky few, it will show us that, too. Have you ever had the experience of meeting someone new when you were with another friend, and you decided that you really liked the other person, whilst your friend had only criticism or disdain for them? This happens owing to perception, which is another way we filter our reality. However, what I am talking about here is at a level deeper than all of that; it is about the attraction of events, people and circumstances, which goes beyond our personal perception filters.

Earlier in this book I discussed a situation where five women spanning five generations in one family had all been raped; the experience travelled from mother to daughter, from mother to daughter, from mother to daughter for several generations. In addition to the hidden loyalties they had towards one another, there was a strong and clear belief system that created the expectation of such experiences that was passed from one generation to the next. These loyalties, combined with a strong belief and expectation, led to each woman's attracting a different perpetrator in a different time and place. This is no coincidence. Scripts are powerful belief systems that hold expectation – what we expect to get is what we get – repeatedly. When we get what we expect, we then stand back and say, "There, you see, it is true!" – and so the cycle goes. Evidence does not create the belief; it is the belief that creates the evidence. As long as we are absorbed with the evidence, we will not be able to change our conviction. As we transform, heal, change and transmute a belief, all the "evidence" in our lives will be likewise transformed.

In order to get there from here, we must become aware of our scripts. Some common belief systems that create scripts include:

- I need the approval of others
- I cannot perform outside of a couple relationship
- My time is not as valuable as other people's time
- I am Jewish, therefore destined to suffer
- I am black, therefore destined to be discriminated against
- Gay relationships never last
- I am (black, of mixed race, a woman, gay, left-handed, etc.), so I will always be seen as a second-class citizen
- I am a woman, therefore destined to be a servant to men
- I am fat, therefore not worthy
- My brother was always the favourite
- My sister is so lucky, she's far prettier than me; beautiful people have all the luck
- My parents always criticised me, therefore it will be difficult for me to succeed at anything
- I am a man, therefore I will always have to work hard in order to support others
- I don't have a university degree, therefore I'll never be recognized for who I am and for what I do
- My credentials define my value as a human being; without them, I am nothing
- Money does not grow on trees
- Success is all about hard work and a lot of luck
- My value is determined by what I own and have
- Very rich people must be crooks in some way
- It's a dog-eat-dog world out there
- Because I am a woman, I must want children; if I don't, then I am not complete as a woman
- As a woman, if I am assertive, I am a "bitch"; men are simply assertive
- As a man, I have to dominate in order to get what I want.

Take a moment to read the list again. Pause by each statement and feel it in your body. How many are true for you? Some of them? Most of them? Scripts can be very subtle, often running in the background on auto-pilot. As we have become accustomed to thinking and believing such things in habitual ways, we are often very unaware that we are doing it. Research has shown us that when we learn a new skill or acquire a new way of thinking, the brain starts to create new neurological pathways. As our accustomed way of thinking is so established, it passes through these pathways unnoticed. We do, however, notice new thoughts, for we have an emotional and physiological response to them. It is not that the old thoughts do not summon these responses; it is that we have become so accustomed that we hardly notice them, if at all. It is a bit like shoes: when they're new, we feel them, and when they're worn in, we hardly notice them. Have you ever read something about quantum physics and exclaimed, "My brain hurts", as you try to wrap your mind around the new and startling concepts? Our "brain hurting" is because the new concepts challenge the existing pathways and accustomed ways we have of thinking; the new concept is literally going against the established grain, and we feel it. Because scripts are habitual ways of thinking that often go unnoticed, it is necessary to become more aware of them. To do this, we need to become aware of how we feel, for our feelings are an excellent barometer for measuring the usefulness of a belief or any given thought. Limiting beliefs are contracting in nature, whereas beliefs that support our natural desires are expansive. A useful way to monitor this is to become aware of your breathing. Again, limiting beliefs are contracting and therefore they constrict the breath; affirming beliefs are expansive and they therefore loosen the breath. In my healing practice, when an individual is able to speak a succinct and defined truth, there is always a relaxed out-breath. Truth relaxes the breath. You can start noticing these feelings now.

As the nature of the soul is to express itself according to the Four Principles of Creation, the tenets upon which the universe is built, when we speak or think that which is contrary to the nature of the soul, we contract; as we speak and think that which is congruent with the nature of the soul, we feel relaxed and expanded. Our breathing and the way our body feels are an excellent guide to the presence of our soul at any given moment, as are our feelings. If something feels bad, it is foreign to our true nature; if it feels good, it is congruent with our true nature. Part of the pathway towards transforming our belief systems is to be in touch with our feelings and to become aware of our body's response to given thoughts. However, it would not be wise to try to monitor all of your thoughts, for there are just too many of them. The most important work is first to identify the beliefs, hidden loyalties, inherited thought patterns and beliefs and to work on deliberately and consciously transforming them into beliefs and thoughts that support your journey from here to there. The more adept you become at identifying your major thought patterns, the more you will become naturally in tune with all your other thoughts, ideas and beliefs. The most important thing to understand is that when you feel expanded, you are on track; when you feel contracted, you are off track.

Watch Out for the Bogeyman

The "bogeyman" refers to those parts of ourselves we try to stuff away or whose very existence we deny. The bogeymen include:

Martyrdom & Self Pity – "Nobody loves me", "I'm the only one who cares", "I always have to do it alone"

Self-Deprecation – "Oh, I'm so stupid", "Oh well, typical me, I'm always the fool", "Perhaps if I apologize for my very existence, they may notice me more"

Stubbornness – "No matter how uncomfortable this is, I'll keep doing it because I am right!"

Arrogance & Shame – "I don't want anyone to see how I really feel, so I'll just pretend. At all costs, they must not see how weak I feel"

Impatience & Control – "I always lose out on everything, so I'll make sure it doesn't happen again"

Greed & Scarcity Consciousness – "I've got to have it all, just in case it all runs out", "There isn't enough, so I had better keep what I have and get even more"

Self Destruction/Sabotage – "Life isn't worth living anyway, it's all hard work for nothing, and then we die, so I might as well just give up", "It's all so pointless, it would be easier to jump off a bridge"

When we become aware of the hidden (and not so hidden) voices in our head, we can begin to embrace our behaviour and response patterns. If you are not certain which of the above belong to you, try asking your closest friends; they will let you know.

It is important to realize that often arrogance and impatience can look very similar. This is how you can tell the difference: You are standing in a queue at the post office and the person behind the counter seems very slow you and the queue is rather long.

Impatience says: "I've got too much to do, maybe I'm losing out on things whilst I stand here, I'll never get it all done, I want what I want NOW".

Arrogance says: "Let me behind the counter, you idiot, I could do your job standing on my head".

Both arrogance and impatience are irritated by the situation at hand, and the response may look similar, but the underlying thoughts are different. The impatient person is staring at their watch every few seconds, whilst the arrogant person is rolling their eyes. Which do you do? Each of these personality traits is linked to a belief system. As you identify and transform the belief, the response pattern will change with time.

The essence of the soul is truth. Therefore, the path of living with the presence of our soul requires truth from us. If you are apt to express a lot of self-deprecation, remember to be gentle with yourself. You did not develop these defence and response mechanisms overnight, so it will take time, courage and willingness in order to transform them.

The Road Less Travelled

Identifying what we want is the easy part; it is getting there from here that is the challenging part for most of us. Not that it is very difficult – it simply takes intention. However, we tend to focus on "here" so much that it becomes difficult to travel on the road to "there". What we say is something like this: "I want to be 'there' because I really don't like being 'here' very much; 'here' is so difficult, 'here' is so boring, 'here' is painful. I'm not 'there' yet because 'here' is holding me back. There is too much 'here' here; I just can't get 'there' quick enough. It is the others that are keeping me 'here', they stop me from getting 'there', it's all their fault, because I really do want to be 'there'".

I call getting "there" the road less travelled, as so many people have trouble identifying what "there" is for them, bemoan their here and now, and therefore switch their focus away from "there" back to "here" – and what we focus on, we get more of. Therefore, when our focus is on "here", "here" remains our destination and we stay put. Similarly, when we do embark on the road less travelled towards the object and subject of our desire, if we constantly look back to our starting point, we cannot see the road ahead of us and it becomes a lot more difficult for us to navigate. Then, lo and behold, we take the easy road back to "here", for that is the place we know best.

Getting from "here" to "there" requires that we make clear statements of where we want to be, without all the "buts" that intersect our statements and serve the purpose of keeping us exactly where we are. The other act of self-sabotage that we often engage in is when we launch our statement of desire and intention but fairly soon afterwards exclaim, "But it is not here yet". I've seen this happen many times with many of my healing clients. They arrive to work on an issue, find a resolution, then exclaim within days that nothing has changed in their lives yet; therefore, by the laws that govern the universe, nothing will. It is of utmost importance that we keep focussed on our goal, for reaching the goal is a journey often involving many steps. We don't have to know all the steps beforehand; they will unfold one at a time. One of the reasons why so many lottery winners end up back where they were financially before they won the lottery, is that they have not taken the inner journey towards wealth. Wealth is a state of being, not a bank balance, so, for the most part, lottery winners end up back where they started, for wealth is not their inner state of being. What we experience externally is merely a reflection of our inner world. If we feel poor, we will be poor; if we feel unresolved with an issue, it will be unresolved; and if we don't understand that all solutions are a journey, we will sabotage their manifestation through our proclamation that nothing is yet happening.

Our world changes according to our vibration and we are conduits for that vibration. We would not expect to be able to pump high-voltage electricity through a regular household piece of wire, would we? Therefore, the journey is to build up the strength and durability of your wiring. The more you build it up with resolving issues of the past and releasing old thought patterns and habits, the greater the vibration you will be able to hold.

Manifesting your desires is a journey. For some things, that journey is almost instantaneous, and for others it takes longer. The journey is an inner journey that manifests itself in time. The more we keep focused on our goals of healing and drawing to ourselves the life condition we want, the shorter the journey will be. We could say that the difference between moving along slowly or steadily on the road towards your desired goal depends on whether you are the eggs or the bacon. The chicken has made a contribution of eggs, but the bacon is totally committed and there is no turning back.

As You Believe, So It Will Be

Part of the work I do with individuals is to assist them in changing their inner picturing of their lives, their family of origin and their relationships, very often with remarkable results. What I encourage each client to do after we have completed a process is to take the new picture and give it a place in their heart and allow it to sink into their soul.

On many occasions a client has come to me regretting that they have a very difficult relationship with one of their parents. They often describe that the parent is critical, challenging and very difficult to get along with. After we have completed our work together, they are able to see a greater truth about their parent and often feel very differently towards them. This transformation of the inner picture is much more successful with those who have decided that it is far better to have peace than to be right. In dozens of cases the client has either called me or has returned for extra work, reporting that their relationship to their parent has totally transformed – the parent is now warm, supportive, gentle and kind towards them – but what intrigues them is that their siblings are still caught up in the old pattern of relationship and continue to bemoan their difficulties.

There are a couple of things happening here. Firstly, when we change our inner picturing regarding reality, reality shifts towards meeting that inner picturing. Secondly, persons who have experienced this phenomenon are no longer anticipating the difficult relationship whenever they call or visit the person in question. As we anticipate a situation ahead of time, we send out the energy of our thoughts into the future and create the situation before we experience it in real time. How often have you planned to visit someone and have spent time beforehand having an inner dialogue that says something like: "If she says this, I'm going to tell her that, and if he dares do this or that, then I'm going say this to them"?

When we change our inner picturing of a relationship, for example, what we are doing is re-writing the unspoken agreements between ourselves and the other. Unspoken agreements say things like, You will behave like this, and I will respond like that. When we have the inner dialogue regarding how bad it is going to be when we visit so and so, we are sending out telepathic airwaves that prepare the other party in advance and we send them the signal that the unspoken agreements are still in place and operational. As we change our inner picturing, we are literally sending the other person the message that the unspoken agreements have changed. As we do this, our pre-paving of the meeting is created out of the anticipation that all will be fine, even joyful, and so, for the most part, the other will agree. Additionally, as we are more than flesh and bones, having an energy body that contains our emotional and mental patterns, as we arrive at our meeting the other is greeted with a different energy coming from us; we are no longer in a state of flux regarding our meeting with them, but calmer, more at peace and more open. Therefore, even though they may be anticipating another challenging meeting with you, as you have changed your inner picturing and therefore your energy exchange with them, there is no longer a resonant match to the old way of responding to one another. This is testimony to the power of changing not only our inner picturing, but also our beliefs about situations and specific relationships. As we believe it, so it is.

It is important to mention here that, through the modality of Family Constellations and trans-generational healing, the power of the family and ancestral energy field is often employed so that things are healed for an entire family, not only for the individual who has participated in a personal process. This is the magic and power of energy. To know more about these specific powerful processes, refer to my two books on the subject: *The Healing of Individuals, Families and Nations* and *The Language of the Soul*.

What we believe creates our experience in so many ways. If you believe that you will be discriminated against for being black, gay, Jewish, a woman, or as someone with a disability, you are pre-creating the situation through sending your belief energy out into the future. Let's say that you are going to an interview and you have already decided that they are particular types of people who work for a particular type of company that is likely to discriminate against you. As you anticipate this, you are sending thought forms and unspoken agreements in advance to the very individuals who will meet you. You are telling them telepathically, "You will discriminate against me, as this is what I expect", and, lo and behold, they agree with your inner picturing and give in to the unspoken agreement. What we anticipate and expect from others is usually what we end up with, for much more of our communication than is verbal, or even physical, is energetic. In essence, as you anticipate discrimination, the other party is also feeling that you are discriminating against them by deciding that they are a certain type of person with particular views, and they will accordingly respond. So the dance has begun, and usually we leave with our dance card empty, for it was all agreed to in advance.

Beliefs not only determine the types of relationships that we have, but they determine every aspect of our lives, whether that be career, health or financial well-being. If we come from a sickly family, we will often manifest illness, partly out of loyalty to the family theme – for it defines whom we belong to – and to those that are sick, but also because we anticipate that it will also be true for us. Our beliefs say, essentially, "My family is sick, therefore I will become sick". When we anticipate good things coming into our lives, they will come; when we anticipate difficulties, our lives will be fraught with them.

The Power of Visualization

For several years I have been using the power of visualization in order to create circumstances and conditions in my life that are pleasing to me. The easiest areas in your life to create change through visualization are the areas where you have the least amount of fear, negative beliefs and resistance.

These are some of the principles I have learnt regarding the successful use of visualization:

- It is important to feel positive and enthusiastic about the subject of your visualization. If, for example, you are visualizing more money coming into your life, but you are feeling fearful of your current financial situation, the visualization will not work for you.

- It is important not to get wrapped up in the details of how the subject of your visualization will come to you. When we do this, we simply get in the way. It is much better to focus on what you want and why you want it than to get bogged down in the "how".

- When visualizing, it is important to focus only on the end result. If you try to visualize whilst focusing on where you are, therefore trying to get to where you want, again your focus will be on where you are and that is what you will get more of.

- Visualization should be fun, not a chore, not a "have to", but as delightful as daydreaming.

Some years ago I was visualizing a new car coming into my life. I knew that the car that I wanted cost a certain amount of money, and I also knew that my clients paid a certain fee and that my workshops earned me a certain income. As I set about my visualization I started to visualize more clients, more workshops with the purpose of generating the income in order to buy the car that I wanted. During my visualization a voice came to me and asked me the following question: "Is it easier for the universe to find you fifty extra clients or just one car?" I was startled, but in that moment I realized that that I was making things far too complicated and was simply getting in the way. The most valuable lesson that I learnt was to leave the details to the intelligence of the universe and to simply visualize the end result. There have been other times when I have wanted to solve a personal issue and have visualized the healing taking place, the end result. What happened in the interim is that by pure "coincidence" I came across a healer or a therapist who specialized in assisting others with the same or a very similar issue to the one I wanted to resolve. When we focus only on the end result, the universe will make all the steps clear with wonderful synchronicity. The greatest downfall with manifesting what you want through the power of visualization is asking the "how" question. We are so accustomed to our lives being structured, seeing that one step follows another and that this detail is followed by that event, and so on, that it often takes practice to disengage our logical and structured mind from the process of visualization.

Here are some typical thoughts that block visualization:

- I want a new home, but how will I pay for it?
- I want a new relationship, but where will I meet him?
- I want to heal, but who will help me?
- I want a better job, but how do I get the qualifications needed?

When we only focus on the end result, the steps, if steps are necessary, will become clear to us, not through the process of trying to work them out, but through synchronicity, which will bring all the people, tools and information required for the next step towards the goal. When you start on the path of visualization, it is better to start with an area of your life in which you feel most confident. As you do this, you will begin to see results quite quickly, and this will then give you the confidence to start working in the areas of your life where you have more doubt or resistance. In order to understand better where you have resistance or doubt, and where your confidence lies, compartmentalise your life into areas such as:

Work/Career
Finances
Relationships
Health
Home.

It is a good practice to journal, writing down what you would like to see in each of these areas of your life, keeping all of your statements positive. *Do not* under any circumstances write down what you don't want! Statements like, "I want a better boss, because my current one makes me miserable", or, "I want a better house because I don't like my neighbourhood", will not work, for such statements only bring you to the place of being focused on what you don't want. Make all of your statements in the affirmative. Also remember that, whilst in theory it is no more difficult to manifest a large mansion than it is to manifest a small cottage, the process of manifestation is a personal journey that brings us growth. For example, if you are visualizing fame and fortune, would you be able to integrate that into your life if it all happened tomorrow or next week? It is not that I am advocating that you should not visualize big things for yourself. Please do, but also understand that you can only bring to yourself that which you are able to *comfortably* hold in your imagination as true. Therefore, if fame and fortune are what you desire, as you visualize this, the steps of your inner journey towards that goal will unfold. If, however, after having visualized fame and fortune, you shout at the universe, "It isn't here yet", then your journey will slow down as your focus once more returns to where you are and away from where you want to be.

Manifestation in itself can be an integral part of our spiritual growth. Whilst much of our focus is on material outcomes, it is important to understand that everything we manifest is a direct reflection of our inner world. Therefore, if it is great financial wealth you wish to attain, the process of developing your inner wealth will begin with that desire, for you must be energetically aligned with all the qualities and maturity you will need in order to hold that wealth in your life. Many of us have difficulty with public recognition, so if your desire is to become a great painter, author, actor, dancer, spiritual teacher, politician, etc., then your journey towards that goal may involve a journey into your inner world of needing approval, your inner critic, and any other belief system or feeling you have that may stand in the way. In essence, conscious creating is a path of individual growth. Very often, when we listen to famous people being interviewed, they talk of their inner journey to where they are standing at the moment. With all the insight into hidden loyalties and inherited belief systems provided in this book, it is my wish that your inner journey towards your dreams and aspirations will be quickened in some way.

When we visualize, we send out a clear thought to the universe regarding the subject of our desire. Images, combined with feelings, are far more powerful than words. One key ingredient to visualization is that it must feel as real as possible, for the more real it feels, the more rapidly we will accept it as a fact in our reality.

Visualization Practice

If you have not visualized before, or not on a regular basis, the following exercises will assist you in gaining practice in making something so real that you accept it as your reality.

Exercise One

Sit in a comfortable chair and ensure that you will not be disturbed for about ten or fifteen minutes. Begin to think about your favourite food. See it, smell it, taste it, and remember the last time you ate it. You will notice with this exercise that your body will respond by producing saliva, which is wonderful. With this exercise you have uncovered a valuable secret to visualization. Your brain does not know the difference between your external reality and your inner reality; both are true! With simple pictures in your mind, your body responds as if they are real. If you really want to test this, imagine cutting your finger with a knife, and see what happens. You will probably grimace and withdraw your finger in defence against the knife. Your brain really does not know the difference.

Exercise Two

Imagine now that you are with someone you feel very close to. See them clearly. Soon, you will be able to remember what they smell like and how you feel when you are with them, and the entire exercise becomes pleasurable.

With the completion of the these exercises, you have learnt how to make your visualizations very real – so real, in fact, that you have fooled your body into thinking that the experience was real. When visualizing your goal so that it feels real for you, so will it be in your life experience and reality.

Preparation for Manifesting through Visualization

When you visualize, it is important that you are well rested and not tired. This will allow you to remain focused on your goal. It is also important that you feel positive about the subject of your manifestation and not in a place of fear regarding its coming or not coming into your life. If you are *feeling* poor in this moment, then trying to manifest greater financial flow will not work for you, so it is important that your feelings match the object of your focus.

When you visualize, whatever the topic may be, visualize in the present tense. In other words, think not that this is something you will have in the future, but that it is happening now. Make the visualization as real as possible, seeing all the details that you can possibly think of. The more you practice visualization, the easier it will become.

When Difficulties Arise

When I have had difficulties in manifesting because I am not feeling very hopeful or positive about the object of my manifestation, I take time out in my garden and remind myself of all the wonderful things I already have, and I consciously begin to think of all the things I am grateful for. I also remember that it is not possible to manifest anything that we don't already have some experience of, so I remind myself that the elements of what it is that I want are already present in my life, and I feel grateful for them. This always brings me into a far better space from which to continue with my visualization work.

How Long?

People often wonder how long a visualization should last. The short answer is, for as long as it feels good and fun to do it. It is important to avoid the trap of believing that the longer you visualize, the more certain it will be that the object of your visualization will come you. A powerful thought with feeling is all that is necessary, and it does not matter if that feeling lasts for ten minutes or thirty minutes. What is important is how often you practice that good feeling space and the powerful thought and image.

A Note on Free Will

As we live in a universe of free will, it is important not to visualize that a specific person gives you what you want – for example, if you have a love interest and want a relationship with a specific person. This is a different matter to visualizing an improved relationship with a person with whom you have difficulty, for in that case, you will perhaps manifest only seeing that person when they are in a positive mood. Trying to manifest that a specific person falls in love with you interferes with free will and will not work. If it is a relationship you want, ask for that, and leave the details to the universe.

Areas of Avoidance

Once you've been visualizing for a while, you may notice that you are focused on only one or two areas of you life. It is important at this stage to ask yourself if you are not working with certain areas because you are happy with what you have, or because they are the areas of the most doubt, limiting beliefs and resistance.

Inner Impulses

A picture paints a thousand words, but it is important to remember that the action part of your life does not come to a halt when you start visualizing. Instead, when you incorporate visualization into your daily life, you will be taking action a little less, and visualizing a little more. Additionally, the actions that you take will begin to feel more guided. In our world we do not manifest out of thin air, but we attract to ourselves the people, objects and circumstances that we desire. Therefore, synchronicity will play a large role in your drawing into your life the object of your desire. You may be sitting in your office or at home one day, musing or imagining your goal to become a fashion designer, and the phone will ring. A friend has called you to invite you to attend a barbecue at her home in a few days. Your inner impulse says a resounding "yes" to the invitation and you accept it without hesitation or even checking your diary. A few days later you go along to the garden party and, through the process of synchronicity, you meet someone who is already a fashion designer who can give you tips on how to start and how to succeed with your desired new career. This is how attraction works. What is most important is that we follow our inner impulses without second-guessing ourselves. When we are able to do this, we are in the flow of our manifestation. The only thing that can get in the way of following our inner impulses is letting logic dictate all of our actions.

Manifesting and the Presence of the Soul

You may be wondering what manifesting has to do with the presence of the soul and why I have dedicated quite a portion of the book to this topic. Here are some points to consider:

- When we become conscious creators and begin to see the results, we deepen our experience of our inherent connection to the creative forces of the universe.

- As we begin to experience synchronicity in our lives, we also begin to understand more fully that the universe is working with us, and not against us.

- Conscious manifestation helps us to tap into the limitlessness of our being and assists us to surpass limitations.

- As we begin to create what we want in our lives, we become more joyful and more peaceful individuals. In order to create what we want, we must develop the qualities of joy, peace and acceptance, and these are soul qualities.

- The path of manifestation teaches us that we get what we focus on in a very direct manner, and it further teaches us about the acceptance of what is and the path of least resistance. We begin to learn why all the things we were against, or tried to exclude, were so present in our lives.

Conscious creation is a growth path in and of itself. Many have seen manifestation and the desire to create and attract things as being materialistic and far from spiritual. However, in my experience, conscious manifesting and creating is very spiritual indeed, by virtue of the inner journey it takes us on. You may very well find that you begin with wanting to attract more money or a new car, which would seem very materialistic indeed. However, as this very process gives you evidence of the grand cooperation of the universe and your inherent power to create your own experience, this knowledge will soon infiltrate every aspect of your life and your manifestation goals will soon move beyond those direct material needs to greater images and goals for yourself. The inner journey is the real gift; the material manifestation is simply the icing on the cake.

CHAPTER NINE

THE POWER OF GRATITUDE

If there is one quality of feeling that stands above all others in bringing us closer to the presence of our own soul, it must be gratitude. Gratitude lifts our spirit in ways that are magical, and it is beneficial for all areas of our lives – health, wealth, relationships, well-being and our ability to create more of what pleases us.

If we have led a life that has left us feeling burdened by our emotions and the stories we have built up regarding the past, then gratitude is an antidote that can be practiced even if we do not naturally feel grateful for many parts of our lives. Gratitude, like anything else in life, is a choice. It is something we can choose to focus on, or not, as the case may be. No matter where you are standing in life at this very moment, there is always something to be grateful for. However, it is a challenge to feel gratitude if one of your core beliefs and feelings is that you are either not worthy or not deserving.

Deserving

Our culture has many beliefs concerning deserving. For the most part we associate deserving with hard work, or we say that a person who has had bad luck and then suddenly gets a break was very deserving. Guilt is one of the enemies of deserving, and so many of us struggle with needless guilt concerning the having and gaining of the good things that bless our lives. Perhaps many of those feelings started as children when we were told to "think of the starving children in Africa" as a command to eat up all our vegetables or to eat everything that was on our plate. Deserving is most often linked to our need for approval from others, for we feel that if we prove ourselves, then we are deserving of better things. However, quite often, deserving is linked directly to our loyalties, hidden or otherwise, to others who have suffered.

Many of our beliefs concerning deserving centre around a work ethic that says that those who toil the most, are most deserving. Many of us would shout with joy on hearing the news that a single mother with four children and three jobs had won the lottery and we would all celebrate her deserving of that prize. However, we may be tempted to feel resentful that a millionaire who already has so much won the prize. This is an indication of our beliefs around deserving, and it is our greatest block to allowing all the good to come to us. Additionally, in Christian cultures we have had centuries and generations of people being taught about the "undeserved kindness of God" – so much so that it has become deeply rooted in our psyche. We have created rules for ourselves that determine who is deserving and who is not, which actions are deserving and which are not, and a myriad of other ways to measure deserving. When we feel undeserving, it becomes a challenge to truly appreciate what we have and allow feelings of gratitude to fill us.

Guilt

Feelings of guilt are the other major blockage to gaining a feeling of gratitude for what we have. We perhaps feel guilty that we have so much when others have so little, or we may feel guilty that others in our family have suffered whilst we enjoy such blessings. It is important to engage in inner work in order to discover the roots of our feelings of guilt. These topics have been discussed more fully in the chapters on Guilt and Remorse and Hidden Loyalties.

Gratitude is the best way to change our mood and feeling about anything. However, a true feeling of gratitude only exists when it is accompanied by a sense of being worthy of what you have. Again, religious abuse has had its role to play in our feelings for gratitude, for we have been told that we *should* be grateful to receive that which we don't deserve.

Gratitude – One Step at a Time

Gratitude can be practiced like any skill we are learning. We don't become champion tennis players overnight, we have to practice. To become skilled at gratitude, we need to make a decision to practice gratitude. You can start with the obvious things in your life, your home, your vehicle if you have one, your garden, your major relationships, friendships, your job or source of income, pets, computer, your ability to buy and read books – the list is endless. One of the best ways to get into the habit of practicing gratitude is to create and keep a Gratitude Diary. To get the most out of your practice of gratitude, take five minutes every day to write down the things for which you are grateful, and be as specific as possible. One day you may simply write that you are very grateful for your car. The next day you may write that you are grateful for the comfort that your car gives you, or the way it makes you feel when you drive it, or the things that your car gives you the freedom to do. It is always beneficial to write down why you are grateful to have certain things, for this will help you to become aware of more things to be grateful for. Another thing that practicing gratitude will do for you is to show you that you already have the elements of the things you are wishing to add to your life – for example, abundance, health, good relationships. They may not be in the quantities you desire, but they are present nonetheless.

Gratitude not only gives you a more positive outlook on your life, it also lifts your spirits, and a lifted spirit is much closer to the presence of the soul than one that feels contracted and lacking in some way. As already discussed in the section on the power of visualization, what you focus on increases; what you believe becomes true for you. Therefore, when you practice gratitude, you are shifting your focus onto the goodness in your life, thereby placing yourself in a position to attract even more. As you think, so you receive; as you feel, so you receive more abundantly. One of the common threads that you will notice among those who have risen to greater wealth or health, is that they are usually very grateful for all that they have. They did not become grateful as they received all they have, but they practiced gratitude on the journey towards the realization of their dreams. So many of us place ourselves in the trap of saying that we will only be happy when this or that happens or when a particular life condition materializes for us. When we do this, we are focusing on the lack of the object of our desire and it remains just out of our reach, just like the donkey and the carrot: as we move ahead, so does the goal. The awareness and practice of gratitude will take you smoothly along your path towards the goal and it is important to practice gratitude every step of the way.

An Empty Life?

Let's say that you are in a place in your life where you do not live in the type of home that you wish to, do not have the relationship that you want, or the health, and your job feels like a soul-destroying dead end. What then? There are *always* things that you can find to be grateful for. Perhaps a tree in your neighbourhood, a good friendship that you have, your ability to walk in the park or to be able to afford a newspaper that has advertisements in it for new and more fulfilling jobs. When your life seems empty, you are mostly focused on not having and are therefore stuck in longing as opposed to desire. As you practice and become aware of gratitude, even for the smallest of things, you will begin to feel a shift. How we feel about things is a choice, and just as depression, martyrdom and self-pity are choices, gratitude is a choice, as well. If you have been stuck in the pattern of feeling self-pity or low self-esteem for several years, it will take consistency on your part to step into the higher vibration of gratitude. Even if it feels forced the first time you get out your gratitude journal (which may just be a scrap of paper, even a paper napkin), I can guarantee that you will sense a shift. Even if that shift is for a mere five minutes, it is a shift in the right direction.

The universe is one of energy; it is the energy that binds all things together. The vibration, or feeling and thought, that you are sending out is bringing to you the circumstances in your life that you are currently experiencing. If you are feeling stuck in a hole of lack, here are some tools you can use in order to change the way you feel:

- rent a comedy or a "feel good" movie
- look up some jokes on the internet
- engage in daydreaming
- go to your local library and get as many motivational books as you can, and read them
- go to a favourite location near where you live (a park, pond, hill, avenue of trees, etc.).

The more you can shift your focus away from the lack that you are feeling, the better position you will be in to practice gratitude and therefore lift your spirits even higher. As you lift your spirits, you will be more in alignment with the presence of your soul and therefore be increasingly open to its inspiration.

Gratitude – The Healer of the Heart

When our heart feels burdened with the loss of what once was, or with the longing for something that feels lacking in our lives, gratitude goes a long way towards healing that heart that feels broken. A broken heart is focused on what once was or what is not present. As we practice gratitude, we will soon experience that there is much for our heart to sing about, and the more we practice, the more our heart will sing. The more our heart sings, the more joyful circumstances we will attract into our lives.

Chapter Ten

SELF-APPRECIATION

On any path of personal and spiritual development and healing, self-appreciation is a key that we must not discard. In fact, it is a key ingredient to leading a more fulfilled life. For many, self-appreciation sounds grandiose or perhaps conceited. However, what it is really all about is giving ourselves permission to be our authentic selves rather than the self we are pretending to be. We are often in the habit of pretending to be many things in order to win favour and approval from others. Ingratiation is the antithesis of self-appreciation. Self-respect, the undeniable companion of self-appreciation, requires of us that we speak and act in integrity and honesty in accordance with our own higher truth – in other words, from the presence of our own soul. When we are truly acting and speaking from our own higher truth, we feel no need to convince anyone of anything. It is the same with self-appreciation, for if we have to convince ourselves of something that is good and worthy about ourselves, then we are not in touch with the deeper and truer version of our self, but only with the layers of inauthenticity and undeveloped aspects of ourselves. Self-appreciation is not a bandage that we can cover negative emotion with. If we have to shout out, "I love myself", in order to convince ourselves that we are worthy, we are simply barking up the wrong tree. Each and every one of us has things we can find to appreciate about ourselves. The key is to start with something that is clearly identifiable and that we accept readily.

At times I have observed that individuals who have been exposed to a lot of self-help material and positive-thinking workshops begin to feel guilty that they do not have a more positive view of themselves. Somehow they have bought into the idea that self-appreciation is a kind of commandment that they must follow and, if they don't, they can no longer consider themselves to be on the leading edge of human development or spirituality. In the past decade I've met a number of people who have liberally offered me all sorts of unasked-for opinions and have made statements like, "Oh, you have a cold, that just means that you don't love yourself enough. You really *should* love yourself more". So now I need to feel guilty for having created my cold because of not loving myself? Whenever new ideas and spiritual insights become dogma, it leads to more ways people can compare themselves to others or feel worse about themselves. It is bad enough that I got a cold, without having to suffer an un-requested lecture from a complete stranger about loving myself more!

Self-appreciation is about finding those things that make us feel better about ourselves when we are able to identify them simply. It is not about identifying qualities that we are supposed to have because some self-help or new spiritual dogma has said that we have to have them. Self-appreciation is also about listening to your own feeling when you are in the company of others. Do you allow others to belittle and criticize you? Do you tolerate being told that you are "less than" in direct and indirect ways? When we develop self-appreciation, such criticism is no longer acceptable to us and we are able to use our sense of self-worth to take ourselves out of the company of such individuals. However, it is important to remember that if the inner dialogue we are having with ourselves is for the most part self-deprecating, then we will continue to attract such behaviour from others. Once we make the conscious choice to become aware of self-deprecation and make changes in how we dialogue with ourselves, we will see how others' communication with us transforms. Our inner dialogue is the message that we send out to the world; if that inner dialogue is primarily self-deprecation, then in essence we are giving permission to others to deprecate us, as well. Once we have made the inner change, it often takes a little time for those to whom we had given unspoken permission to criticize us, to change their manner of communication, and we may need to inform them gently that this is no longer what we want. At first, this can create tension in relationships and friendships, for the other has simply been going along with the unspoken rules of the relationship that have been agreed upon, and through your inner shift you have now changed the rules of engagement. Sadly, some friendships and relationships will need to end and it is important to remember that you do not need the other's love or approval in order to feel good about yourself. Feeling good about yourself is your job; it is not the job of another to do that for you. Communicating new sets of rules to others is best done gently, for when we become defensive or angry it simply creates a power struggle. It is important to understand that we cannot blame others for our lack of self-esteem or for the pattern of self-deprecation, for it has been our chosen response to them and to the words they have spoken that has created our pattern.

> *"...Everything can be taken from a man but one thing:*
> *the last of the human freedoms – to choose one's*
> *attitude in any given set of circumstances,*
> *to choose one's own way."*

> Viktor Frankl,
> *Man's Search for Meaning*

When others criticize, belittle or demean us in some way, they are simply communicating from their own view of themselves, for when we feel good about ourselves, we naturally do not attempt to make others feel bad. Therefore it is important not to take things personally, even when the words of another feel like a personal attack. The more authority we give the opinions of others, the more negative emotion we will feel and the more intense our sense of suffering will become. Our levels of unhappiness simply match our level of agreement to it; we are as unhappy, or as happy, as we believe and allow ourselves to be.

One of the difficulties with embracing self-appreciation is that self-appreciation has often been confused with arrogance. We have heard others say things like, "Goodness, look at him, he really loves himself! He think's he's the cat's whiskers". Statements like these are used to describe people we perceive to be conceited, arrogant and perhaps showing a sense of superiority. Through many centuries of religious dogma that has taught us that we are nothing more than lowly "sinners", self-appreciation has received a bad rap and we have been encouraged to keep ourselves small, insignificant and humble. But what is humility? Humility is about respecting the greatness, the fate, the uniqueness and the presence of others. When we are in self-appreciation, we not only respect these things about ourselves, we naturally have the same respect for others. One of the great contradictions about modern life is that we are often expected to be great, to succeed, to become champions and to do our best, and yet we are not expected or indeed allowed to announce our success in polite company.

We have the power to choose our feelings at any given moment. A negative response to the words of others is simply a conditioned response, something we have been doing for a long time. However, like any habit, it can be changed. How we feel about ourselves is defined only by us, not by another. The moment we allow how we feel about ourselves to be defined by another, we not only give our power away, but we also create a chasm between ourselves and the presence of our soul. At times it is very challenging not to feel overwhelmed when the world and everyone in it seems to be telling us that we are not good enough, not intelligent enough, not beautiful enough, not, not, not...the list goes on. Many of these messages are subtle – for example, a media image that tells us what beauty is or what success is. In such cases, it is very clear that we are telling ourselves the message through our interpretation and acceptance of the message. In essence, it never really is about the other, it is always about us and what we choose to believe. What we choose to believe is already present in one form or another within our consciousness, which is why it is so easy to accept such messages with very little resistance. Just as we cannot desire something that we don't already have some experience of, so we cannot accept a negative image if we are not already holding a similar negative image about ourselves.

Feedback

It is very important that we are able to discern the difference between positive feedback and criticism. As a rule of thumb, if the feedback is communicated in a gentle, loving and supportive way, then it is worth our consideration. None of us is ever beyond reproach, for we are not perfect human beings. Being open to suggestion and guidance from others is of great benefit. When offering guidance and suggestions, it is advisable always to ask permission first, instead of simply offering opinions wildly.

Exercise

Take a piece of paper and begin to list everything that you appreciate about yourself. Divide the piece of paper into four sections or columns and identify things that you appreciate about yourself in the following areas:

My Body	*My Personal Qualities*
Myself as a Friend	*Myself as a Partner/Lover/Spouse*

Once you've identified a positive aspect of yourself, add why. *Some examples:*

• *I love my hands, because they are strong (dainty, beautiful, they allow me to play the piano, etc.)*

• *I appreciate my generosity towards others, because it feels good to reach out and connect with others*

Once you've identified the aspects of yourself that you appreciate, take a moment to look at your entire list and underline any qualities that you would like to develop further. In doing this, you will shift your focus onto what is good and wonderful about you whilst creating opportunities for greater growth and expansion. An example:

• *I would like to develop my humour further as it's such fun and feels good when I laugh with others*

Now take another piece of paper and write down the things that you do not appreciate about yourself in the same life areas previously used. However, instead of focusing on what you do not appreciate about yourself, turn it around – create a statement of how you would like it to be. Some Examples:

• *I hate my thighs / I want to appreciate my legs and thighs more*

Exercise, continued

• *I dislike the fact that I nag my partner so much / I want to be more appreciative of my partner's ability to take care of herself/himself*

When we turn what we don't appreciate about ourselves into positive statements, our focus shifts. Shifting what we don't like about ourselves is simply a matter of shifting focus. When we focus on what we don't like, we simply get more of it. When we focus on what we do like, we get more of that!

Humour

Don't take it all so seriously! Piety simply makes us morose and rather boring. The path of spiritual and personal development is an adventure and, if we so choose, we can have fun with it. The next time you catch yourself lecturing another, spouting some dogma or a list of do's and don't's, just imagine that you are watching yourself doing it and have a good old belly laugh; realize just how ridiculous you are being and say to the other, "Sorry, that's how I used to think and behave", and laugh out loud! Being serious all the time isn't going to get you a better spot in the angelic hierarchy when you die; what it will do is make your life rather glum. Having a defined intention towards our personal and spiritual development is not the same as being serious to the point of squeezing all the playfulness out of our lives. We can be serious and committed regarding our intent, but that does not mean that we have to lead life as if we were the nuns and monks of old, walking around in sackcloth. Laughter and the ability to laugh at ourselves is a great way to release tension, open the heart, and begin to see the world differently. Stand-up comedians are able to make audiences laugh because they talk about what is very familiar to us all, and that is what makes it so funny. There is so much that we do and think and ways we react that are rather ridiculous, especially when done with so much seriousness that it squeezes every last drop of joy out of life. Being passionate about what we do and being serious about it are two different things. When we are passionate, we are speaking and acting from the presence of our own soul; when we are serious to the exclusion of all fun, then we are stuck in the shoulds, shouldn'ts and piety. Piety shuts off all access to inspiration and to our greatness.

CHAPTER ELEVEN

SPIRITUAL PRACTICE

Once we have encountered the presence of the soul, we understand that intransigent dogma has no place in the realm of the soul. The essence of the soul is acceptance. Therefore any spiritual teaching that exhorts us to view other spiritual practices as wrong, or encourages us to see the world as split into that which is more spiritual and that which is less spiritual, lacks the essence of soul. There are many who consider themselves to be on a spiritual path, who have the tendency carve up their lives into those activities which are spiritual and those that are not. However, when we are living the presence of our soul and are therefore motivated by what feels good and joyful, we bring soul essence into everything we do, whether we are a cook, an architect, a mother, a banker, a dentist or a gardener. The essence of spirit is one of allowing and acceptance, and also one of joy and appreciation. Even though we are living in a renaissance of spiritual awareness, the so-called "New Age", we are still living with the residual impact that organized religion has had on our psyche. The organized religions in the world have imbued us with notions that tell us that if we do things in a certain way and believe in certain doctrines, we will be assured a better place after we die. These belief systems are as alive today as they ever were, even though we are no longer marching *en masse* to churches (no pun intended) to listen to all the doom and gloom and to be told that we are sinners. As these beliefs had a stranglehold on humanity for scores of generations, the beliefs have easily been passed down to us today. Many people today who have embraced new forms of spirituality do not yet understand that, for the most part, they have simply exchanged one set of dogma for another. Today you will find individuals and groups of people that, instead of believing in hellfire, will try to convince you that all of your bad luck and suffering is a result of your wrongdoing or wrong thinking in a previous incarnation.

Additionally, just as the Church was once the sole authority on spiritual teaching and doctrine, many people today have transferred the same authority onto their guru, spiritual teacher, or even the utterances of a channeled entity, re-creating religious dogma all over again. If we are the creators of our own experience and are sovereign entities in our own right, then any spiritual path that prescribes a rigid doctrine is therefore incongruent with the essence of the soul.

In recent years, as many people have become disillusioned with life in the developed nations of the world, indigenous spiritual practices have been increasingly sought out and accepted. It is my belief, though, that much has been over-romanticized regarding both the originating cultures and their practices. In my view, this romanticism is born out of two things: Eurocentric culture's feelings of guilt towards indigenous cultures and our exploitation of them; and the disillusionment we have felt with technologically-driven lives where science and the acquisitions of "things" have been more dominant than spirituality. This movement towards expressions of indigenous spirituality is indicative of the spiritual void that many are feeling in the developed nations of the world. Whilst there is great value in these spiritual practices, I believe that they take us further away from who we are, rather than closer, for as humans, not only are we souls, but we are also members of a family that has existed for countless generations. It is my belief that we are better able to find peace when we also include the spiritual traditions of our own ancestors, rather than looking towards the spiritual traditions of others as being better than our own. Each of the world's major religions, including Christianity, has an esoteric expression that is closer to the essence of soul than the dogma of its mainstream expression that we are more familiar with. Additionally, if we are of European ancestry, there is a wealth of spirituality within the druidic and Celtic religions of our more distant ancestors. As I was raised as a Catholic, I still find great peace and serenity when entering an old chapel in Europe. Many of these chapels have stood for a thousand years or more and are imbued with the prayers of countless generations. Now, when I gaze upon the statue of Mary and light a candle at her feet, I think of the countless generations of women in my own bloodline who gave birth to the next generation and who selflessly nurtured their own children, and so on, so that I could have this life experience. At times, I see Mary as representing the earth itself, a mother who is blameless and who holds us within and on her body, sustaining us; at other times, I see her as the divine feminine principle that gave birth to the Christ, the heart of humanity, for it is the feminine that has hitherto been emotionally rather than intellectually centered. All of these meanings we can gain from the religion of our ancestors and from our own spiritual upbringing. When we look at all religions, leaving out the dogma, each of them has great value in their symbolism and in their basic teachings – "honour thy mother and father" is one that immediately comes to mind – so they all provide encouragement to pay homage to our ancestors.

As the essence of the soul and its presence are felt through gratitude, acceptance, allowing, joy, well-being and abundance, any spiritual practice that expresses one or more of these qualities will assist you in focusing even more on the soul qualities that you wish to develop in your day-to-day life. My advice is to be open to other spiritual teachings and practices and take those that help you most to experience the soul qualities that you seek. Your spiritual practice may be to sit in meditation and recount quietly to yourself everything that you are grateful for, or to sit in front of an altar and give thanks to your ancestors and to remember the dead with gratitude in your heart, or to recite a traditional Jewish prayer, say the rosary, or incorporate some other element that expresses the spirituality of your ancestors who may have come from Africa or elsewhere. There is no real right or wrong with this, as long as it feels good in your heart and connects you to the qualities of the soul.

CHAPTER TWELVE

REINCARNATION

Many spiritual traditions around the world uphold the notion of reincarnation, including the more esoteric expressions of the world's main religions such as Christianity, Judaism and Islam. There are many different beliefs and teachings concerning reincarnation, however. Many traditions teach that reincarnation is a path of evolution, and the teachings are often infused with concepts such as:

1. Reincarnation serves the purpose of allowing the soul to evolve to a better/higher state of being;

2. If one fails in one's evolution though misconduct or evil deeds, you will return either to a life of suffering or as a lower life form;

3. Once the path of reincarnation is complete, the soul remains in a state of eternal bliss.

Whilst I certainly do subscribe to the concept of reincarnation and believe that I have personal evidence of that, I do not subscribe to any of the notions I have mentioned above. Whilst reincarnation can be seen as a path of evolution, I do not believe that it is designed in such a way that earth-bound souls need to either improve or prove themselves worthy of a higher state of being, as if earth life were some sort of test or universal boot camp. If we existed prior to this life experience, then we would have existed in the state of being pure energy, so how is it possible that we would need "improving" or betterment through experiencing life on earth? If we are on the "wheel of karma" in order to become worthy of nirvana, how then did we become unworthy in the first place? It simply makes no sense to me.

Through my many "mystical" experiences, I have begun to understand that the *raison d'être* for all life is simply experience.

As souls we have been present in many different planes of existence and in each one we have sought experience. Furthermore, souls are the medium through which the universe becomes conscious of itself. As we are driven by experience, and one of the Four Principles of Creation is creation itself, we seek to know ourselves through the extension of what we have created, attracted to ourselves and manifested. As pre-incarnated souls we saw the earth and all it has to offer as yet another reality out of countless realities in which we can experience ourselves in many different forms, under many different conditions, in many varied environments. As earth is a place of contrast – for we have many opposite poles or dualities present here: good, bad; up, down; light, dark; etc. – we have also noticed the contrast between levels of awareness, maturity and consciousness when we look at our fellow human beings. We have made decisions regarding the "more evolved" and the "less evolved", which in turn has led us to view consciousness as having linear movement; this implies a beginning point, a middle point and an end point. The problem with this view, whilst being abundantly clear to most aware observers, lies in the interpretations that have been placed on the meaning and purpose of both the beginning and the end points.

Let me give you an analogy of how the soul views reincarnation. Let us say that after having mastered lacrosse, volleyball and surfing you decide, for you are an experience-seeking being, that you would now like to master tennis. Naturally, even though you do have sporting skills that have been developed in other areas of experience and play, you would not start your foray into tennis in the championship league but would likely start with all the other beginners. Once you've progressed through the game and have developed your skills, you may want to experiment with playing doubles, trying your skills out with lawn tennis and other forms of the sport. However, once you've mastered the game, would you then sit on the sidelines with your championship medals and do nothing further? Simply sit in bliss, marvelling at your own success? There are other tournaments to play in, other opponents, and more varied levels of skill. Perhaps you would decide to teach tennis professionally, or to try polo or table tennis.

Reincarnation is like learning how to play tennis. We were involved in getting to know ourselves and our skills in other sports (realities) and, as naturally experience-seeking beings, we gazed upon the earth plane and thought, "now that's different, that looks like fun", and off we went to play the game called "Life on Earth". In my view, looking at the variations in consciousness and awareness in the world's population is the same as looking at several different games of tennis involving players at different levels of experience and skill. Time and practice are what usually develop skill in the game. However, there are those who seem to have a natural skill for the game, and they are likely to be those who have mastered many other sports. If you are, say, a painter and decorator who has never played a sport before, you may expect that your progress will be a little slower than it would be for one who has mastered other sports to championship levels. So it is with souls. The difference between young souls and old souls is really about how long they have been at this game called Earth Life, their previous experience in similar environments, and their intention behind entering the sport. Not everyone has the same intention or goal. Some want to dabble, some want to master, others want to go on and teach others how to play the sport, whilst others simply play it for the exercise, and still others play one or two games and decide that they much prefer swimming; tennis simply isn't for them.

What I'm saying with all of this is that the purpose of reincarnation and being here is not about being placed or imprisoned on the wheel of karma until we get it right or are good enough to frolic in other worlds, for we have been in those other worlds already. This is a place that we choose to experience for the sake of experience. My essential message with all of this is to encourage you to lighten up and relax more regarding the whole purpose and meaning of being on planet earth. This is not a school we are stuck in until some higher authority decides that we may graduate or are good enough to move on. We ourselves make that decision. Religion has focussed mostly on the external authority of God, or on its own authority regarding doctrine. This alternate view brings all the authority and free will back to where it belongs, with us. The dominant view of souls as being choreographed by a larger external authority has contributed to limiting views of reincarnation that place it in the realm of "good actions bring reward, bad actions bring suffering". Whilst it is true that "bad" actions bring consequences not to our liking, there is no judge or jury; we are those, for we are the creators of our experience. Imbued with the creative essence of All That Is, we learn through our many lifetime experiences what feels good and what doesn't, and eventually we cease doing all the things, even having all the thoughts, that bring us more discomfort.

Through my own inner explorations I have, however, experienced that we do indeed make some agreements before coming here. Just as with tennis, we may sign up for an entire season, or for a certain number of games, or even make agreements to play with certain other tennis players. When we join a tennis tournament, it is expected that we will see out the entire season until the end of the tournament and not drop out halfway through, so we make a commitment. As we approach earth, we likewise make agreements with others and primarily make an agreement with ourselves to remain in the Earth Life game until we have reached a level of skill and expertise that we are satisfied with, or until we are satisfied with our experience here.

When I talk of levels of skill and expertise, what could that mean? There are certain principles that underpin the workings of the universe. These principles are the Four Principles of Creation – Love, Health & Well-being, Abundance and Creativity. As the Earth Life game is preset to a skill level of "difficult", owing to its containing the illusion of separateness, our challenge within this particular sophisticated holographic game is to succeed in expressing ourselves according to the Four Principles – that is, despite the illusions. We seek to live a life here that is filled with Well-Being, Abundance, Health, and the knowledge that we create our own reality. This is one of the greatest challenges, as life within this holographic representation of reality seems to be filled with the evidence that the Four Principles are not natural laws and that we live in a world governed by pure chance.

We can imagine two souls getting together to have a chat after a few lifetimes on earth. It might go something like this:

Sue: So, how did your last earth experience go for you?

Bob: Quite well, actually. I got the Abundance thing down very well, I created a lot of wealth and all was well in that area of my life.

Sue: And the rest?

Bob: Er...not as enjoyable. I only experienced Abundance in the area of material goods and money; my relationships were a travesty.

Sue: Oh dear, so what are you going to do now?

Bob: Well, I did decide that I was going to master this game, so I'm off for another go. How well did you do?

Sue: Hhmm, not much better. I worked on my skill of determination and got very good at not giving up, so I was pleased at that, but I failed miserably at allowing others to be. I became a little bit of a tyrant.

Bob: Oh dear, so what now?

Sue: Well, I've decided to be born into a culture that is rule-bound, and I hope that this will stimulate me to discover the freedom to be and let be at many more levels.

Bob: Cool, that sounds like a good plan. I'm planning to be born into a very poor family so that I can discover what love is without all the money. However, I'm hoping that the poverty will stir in me the desire to create wealth again and that I'll take with me the lessons of love and cooperation that I plan to learn whilst living in poverty.

Sue: Goodness, Bob, that's quite a challenge!

Bob: Well, you know me, just like any typical soul, totally bored unless I've got something to do, but I am so glad that I'm out of the stage of creating mayhem. Mind you, that life as Genghis Khan was fun though....

Sue: Yes, I remember. How did you resolve that one?

Bob: Well, I gave myself quite a few setback points after that, no one forced it onto me. I wanted to experience being born into a family that had been devastated by certain events so that I would inherit limiting belief systems regarding power, force and dominance. I did quite well; it all seemed so much more satisfying to crawl my way out of the setback points. I learnt so much about myself.

Sue: Didn't you bite off a little more than you could chew?

Bob: No, I don't think so. I've been at this long enough to know that I can deal with setback points. One day in the future I would like to create a leadership role all over again and see how well I do.

Sue: That sounds like a good plan. Anyway, I'm off to an incarnation as a girl from a conservative background who wants to become a corporate executive. I've always wanted to find out how well I'd do at the game of sexism. Wish me luck!

Bob: Goodness, I've not even been there yet. I hear that some of the other souls have played that game a hundred times or more and still haven't managed to master getting out of the pre-programming of sexism. Good luck with that one!

Sue: Thanks, Bob.

"Setback points" refer to the conditions that we choose to be born into, not the conditions that are predestined to dominate an entire lifetime, unless of course we are unable to transform the beliefs we inherit as we set the level of setback points at the beginning of the new game. Setback points are not punishment, but rather challenges we set for ourselves in order to improve our skills. The soul thrives on experience and seeks to master each experience it enters into. The soul is grateful to those already incarnate who agree to allow it to join their biological family through the process of incarnation. The soul knows in advance the belief systems, the traumas and conditions that have affected and are present in the biological family and therefore selects a family that is in alignment with its own personal goals. From the perspective of the soul, each biological life is a great and valuable gift, for it provides the conditions the soul seeks in order to advance in the game and improve its skills.

When we consider reincarnation, especially if we have had a challenging and difficult childhood, we may ask with dismay, "Why did I choose these parents?" We ask this with dismay and a touch of martyrdom only when we have not yet embraced our fate. It is only when we embrace our fate that we are able to do something with it. All of the negative conditions and programming we have received can be consciously used to launch desires that are the opposite of what we started with. However, our desire to create more joyful conditions is impaired when we bemoan the start of our journey. This process has great value, as we need to work at honing our skill and rise above the negative. When we are able to do this, we feel great satisfaction and a deep sense of inner peace comes forth from our soul. One of the most difficult concepts for most people to embrace is that our soul comes forth into our physical body just for the experience and for how it can develop its own awareness and creative skills within this reality. The difficulty arises when we are unable to see how living a difficult and painful childhood may be of benefit to anyone, not least ourselves. What the soul seeks is to experience itself as creator within the physical world. The physical world presents unique challenges and, essentially, if we can master the art of allowing and conscious creation within the physical world, we can do it anywhere.

When we look at challenges such as sexual abuse, physical abuse, congenital defects or childhood diseases, it is challenging to see what value could be gained from such experiences. However, we only really need to look at individuals who have risen above such life experiences and notice some of the qualities they have developed – courage, determination, acceptance, allowing, compassion, love, for example. All of these qualities are soul qualities. As the soul understands that it does indeed create its own experience and reality, it seeks to discover itself under circumstances that are challenging, for this is how the soul gains growth and experience. The soul does not see suffering; it only sees experience and what can be gained through all experiences, whether or not we deem the experience to be of value. It is not that the soul forces suffering upon us throughout our lives. Our souls only choose the initial conditions of each life we have led, in order to discover how we will rise above challenges and use the natural laws of the universe to transform conditions such as pain into love, resistance into allowing, poverty into wealth, lack of opportunity into opportunities, sickness into health, and so forth. As duality presents us with stark contrasts, the soul seeks to use the contrast as a springboard so it may rediscover the greater part of itself whilst present in the physical world.

Sometimes you may wonder what the point is to reincarnation if we have little or no memory of our past lives. Well, it is the same as with the current life we are leading. Just as we do not remember everything about our very early childhood, the experiences nevertheless remain with us, along with the knowledge and what we have gained. Just as we would not wish to focus on all of our childhood memories when we wish to move forward in life, so it is for us as souls. It is my belief that clear and constant past-life memories would only confuse us and diffuse the focus of this lifetime. We can barely remember who were at the age of four and only have snippets of images, some memories and perhaps some feelings, and so it is for past life experiences.

There are two ways of considering the amount of lifetimes we have here on earth. One view is that, because the vibration of the physical world is so dense, it takes time and a lot of experience in order for us to rise above that and begin once again to experience ourselves as souls and gain the memory and knowing of our innate ability to create consciously. The other view is that, because this is such a diverse planet of great contrasts and choices, the soul is driven towards and motivated by more experience. There are virtually unlimited ways in which we can experience ourselves on earth. We are growth- and experience-seeking beings with knowledge of the self being the primary motivation and goal, and earth is a very attractive proposition for any soul wishing to achieve growth and experience. Older souls are not immune to difficulties and challenges; it is how a soul processes the experience that indicates maturity. As humans, the younger we are, the more drama we tend to create when challenges come our way; when we get older, we tend to have a little more perspective. So it is with the varying degrees of soul awareness and consciousness present on the planet today.

Levels of soul awareness are neither good nor bad, higher or lower, better or worse. If we say that the awareness of an older soul is "better" in terms of intrinsic value as opposed to simply acknowledging its experience, it becomes the same as deciding that kindergarten children and teenagers at high school are somehow less than a university student who is far older and has received more education. We live on a planet whose population has a very broad mix of soul ages. Some are relatively new arrivals, whilst others have been around a number of times. One of the great challenges for older souls is to be in acceptance of the world as it is and to be in a place of allowing when it comes to the perceived ignorance and immaturity of those around them. Ideally, an old soul simply wants to sit under a tree and read a book, whilst at the same time wanting to ask all of the younger souls to kill one another a little more quietly so as not to be a distraction. Older souls are far more introspective than those with less experience. As older souls have gained so much experience, they are more inclined to be introspective rather than choosing intense experience. Older souls that may have set themselves the task of being teachers of any given philosophy are likely to have chosen intense childhood experiences; however, the intensity will diminish the older they get. On the other hand, much younger souls may continue to create intensity for the entire duration of their lives. Another challenge for older souls is fitting in to the world at large and also finding a clear path. As older souls have had so many incarnations, they are inclined to have many areas of expertise which can lead to much indecision regarding career and the expressions of their life's work. As an older soul has pretty much done it all, they can do many different things and tend to get bored rather quickly. A typical old soul will have their fingers in many different pies, which often goes against the societal norm. The other bane for older souls is that they often sit around musing and creating worlds and corporations in their head, for they understand that that is where reality starts, and they may not actually take much action.

For the older soul, life can seem very challenging at times. It can feel as if we are busy with our doctorate in life and have been forced to attend a local high school full of teenagers and children that can bring us to the edge of insanity. We teeter between having a deeper understanding of the others and wanting to mow them all down with a machine gun. This is the challenge of the older soul – acceptance of what is. We begin to learn at a much deeper level that our resistance to what is simply creates more of what is, and that the path of acceptance is indeed the path to peace in this multifaceted reality we find ourselves in. Old souls seek peace and cooperation at all costs. But they are not strangers to preaching – preaching being yet another symptom of resistance to what is. The key to mastering life on this earth is to sit back and say, "It is what it is", and realize that we do indeed have the power to create the exact experience we wish to have.

Whether or not you subscribe to the idea of reincarnation, the model is useful as a guide to understanding the differing levels of awareness on the planet and how we can best deal with a world of people who often think and feel very differently to the way we may think and feel. The essential message with this chapter on reincarnation is to state that the circumstances of our early experience of life are not intended to either punish us or bring some sort of retribution for past-life deeds. It is all experience, and those experiences can motivate us to dig deeper and find the greater, more radiant part of ourselves – or we can allow ourselves self-pity and so sink even deeper into darkness and shrink from the presence of our souls. If there exists a higher authority in the person of God, I can imagine that omnipotent being asking us this: "I gave you a fate; what did you do with it?" How would you answer?

Each life presents us with choices. We can either shed the fears we hold regarding our own greatness and allow our inner light to shine, or we can succumb to wanting and needing to find approval and acceptance in a world that often feels foreign to our true inner selves, thereby hiding our light under a bushel. We can pretend to be happy in relationships when we are not, or force ourselves to feel safe in careers and jobs that do not feed our soul or allow us to experience our unlimited abilities and natural talents. We can choose to follow our logic when every fibre of our being is urging us to do something else, or we can place to one side our fear of criticism and of not fitting in and simply choose what feels good and natural for us to do. Living a life in the presence of our soul is all about the choices we make, how we communicate to others and to ourselves, and how true we are to our own inner impulse to stretch towards greatness. Exceptional human beings are those who have left fear behind and who live their truth no matter what.

This is the path of the soul. When we meet such individuals, we love to bask in their light, for they represent our deeper yearning. We admire and respect them and are often in awe of them. However, they are not anything special; they are simply being themselves. They are living in the presence of their own soul and that is totally normal for them. When we stand in awe of such individuals, which is natural, we often create in our own mind the concept that living and breathing the soul as they do is a special gift that only the very talented can achieve. When we realize that they are simply being who they are, we can then accept that the goal of living, being and doing as it is our own nature to do, is achievable. All we need to do is remain true to who we are and express our essence.

FINAL CHAPTER

KEY POINTS

All the things I have written in this book are things that I absolutely know to be true – not because they make logical sense to me, but because I have experienced them to be true in my everyday life. I do not know all of the answers to life, and it seems to me that the more I know, the more questions I seem to have. As my perspective broadens, I become aware that there is much, much more to understand and to live. I am by no means a master of all of the principles I have written about in this book. Some things I am close to mastering at times, and other things I still need to remind myself of on a regular basis. What I do know to be true is this: once you understand the truths in this book and begin to put them into practice, your life will change for the better. Some things you will be good at instantly, and others you will need to work at. Each of us is a work in process.

When we live unfulfilled and empty lives, or lives that are filled with the drama of living on planet earth, we often hope that, once we are done with this life, we will retreat to some nirvana or heaven somewhere and live in eternal bliss. Whilst that notion is very appealing, it simply goes against the nature of the soul, for we are growth- and experience-seeking beings. A millennia or two in nirvana could be rather boring, and some of us might be bored after just a hymn or two in a heavenly choir of angels. "What next?" we will shout, and off we will go again, seeking even more experience. Some have seen reincarnation as a process in which we get good enough to be somewhere other than on this clod of real estate floating in circles around our sun in the vastness of the galaxy and the universe. However, I have come to learn that we are simply here for the experience. There are so many good things here on planet earth.

Over the years I have often thought of the words of the Lord's prayer, "on earth as it is in heaven". I believe that part of our purpose here is to create with the same freedom that we experienced before coming to this earth. Rather than being a planet of dunces who need to improve themselves before moving on to better and better realms of existence, we are courageous, experience-seeking souls who set up a reality (or a game) that poses more challenges than usual, a little like setting the skill level on a computer game. I have experienced that my soul not only chose to come to this place, but had great joy and excitement in doing so. I used to ask "why" all the time, especially when I saw this planet of our as a less-than-good place to be. However, as I have healed many of my emotional wounds and have cleared out a quantity of my own illusions, my view has become different. Now when I ask "why", I usually just tell myself, "because", and I'm happy with that. For me, the search for the Holy Grail has been something of a cosmic joke, for it has been right under our noses all the time – quite literally, for it is nestled comfortably and eternally in our hearts. The quest is not to find the secret that God or the gods have in mind for us, it is not to uncover the hidden meaning to it all; it is simply to listen to our hearts. Listening to my heart simply means doing what feels exciting, expansive, fun and joyful to do, and to do it all with gratitude – it really doesn't get more complicated than that. The basic secret to life is that we create our own reality and that we are connected to everyone and everything, All That Is, at all times, no exception. The distance that separates us from our soul, or from God, is the distance we have created ourselves, owing to our perception of who we are, how deserving we are, and where and to whom we belong. God is not out there, the soul is not a mystery; God and the soul are here right now, within us and around us.

On my path of healing, I have discovered that in this physical experience I am first and foremost a human being, and that is a good thing. As a human being, I have attributes and a physical body given to me by my parents and by my ancestors. In this reality, at least, I belong to my ancestors and the ancestors are a gateway to that which appears greater than myself, to Source itself. I have experienced that there is a wealth of love, experience and knowledge buried in the repository of human experience and consciousness, and that we can tap into this when we move to a place of being in total acceptance of our human experience. So many of us have experienced pain as we grew up and suffered the vagaries of family life and the traumas than went with it, and we have perhaps looked towards things spiritual for our answers. In my experience, however, many of the answers lie within human history and the history of our family. The presence of the soul is felt not only on some spiritual plane of existence, but also directly within the bonds that bind human beings together.

I never expected to witness some of the secrets to the universe being revealed through studying and experiencing family dynamics, but, the more I looked, the more apparent they became. Evidence of the soul was in abundance and the confirmation that we do indeed create our own reality through our thoughts and feelings was also clear to see. Even with all of this being evident to me, though, I still have some unanswered questions – mainly, why is it that in one family one child can be very burdened by the events of the past that entangle the family whilst another child within the same family is scarcely touched? After several years of working with others, I have come to the conclusion that certain questions are the domain of the soul and that it is not my business to pry into those matters which are personal to the souls in question. Of course, there are those who will try to quickly explain this with the concept of karma and reincarnation. Even if that is the case, though, is it our right to know about another? Should certain matters remain a mystery, or private? Suffice it to say that I do not possess all of the answers and I see my job as one of assisting others when specifically asked to do so, using the knowledge and experience I currently have.

I feel that there is great danger when we interpret the heavier burdens that some souls may have as being connected to karma, unless we are in a place of total compassion and acceptance. When we try to make these distinctions we may be tempted to make other judgements, which in my view goes totally against the very quality of the soul. I have come to see certain things as simply being fate. Fate is not something that we can argue with, and it is neither fair nor unfair, it simply is. From a human perspective, that is a very liberating way of looking at fate. From the soul's perspective, a given fate is chosen, for its own reasons, and I do not consider it my work to try to figure out why. My fate is my business, and your fate is yours. We can assist one another to heal the results of any given fate, but we cannot truly know the absolute reason for the existence of another's fate. Although we can see the origins and workings of fate within family systems, why a soul has chosen that remains a mystery to me. I have some clues and ideas about my own fate, but it takes a great deal of sensitivity and self-awareness to get to the point of knowing one's fate and the reasons behind it. Fate is not to be confused with pre-destiny, for we all have free will; fate is simply the hand of cards we are dealt (or have chosen) as we come into this physical world.

My gifts to you with this book are some insights into the nature of the presence of the soul, how to become aware of it and how to practice and live it. What I also offer you are tools that will put you on the unfolding path of a more magical and joyful life.

Recap

Many of the concepts in this book may be totally new to you, or perhaps they are very familiar but are being presented from a perspective that is new to you. When we consider the presence of the soul, it is very easy for us to look upwards towards a spiritual realm rather than to look more closely at the human domain. What I hope to have demonstrated in this book is that many of the elements of soul, soul qualities and indeed universal or metaphysical principles and laws can be seen, felt and experienced simply by looking at the family of humanity. There is much honour, grace and humility in bowing to one's fate and much evidence of the deep bonds of love that we have for one another as it becomes evident that we frequently create our own suffering out of loyalty to other family members and to our ancestors.

The soul, which is inclusive of all things, is evident everywhere we look, when we look with the eyes of understanding and knowing. I am reminded so often of the deeply moving moments when clients have reverently bowed to the fate of their ancestors, feeling a deep sense of gratitude that the ancestors' suffering had led to the gift of their life and its circumstances. In these moments, it feels as if the hand of God is present and there is a stillness that is ten thousand times louder than the quietest whisper of an angel, a stillness that is so profound that we can only stand in awe and gaze upon the presence of an individual's soul as they touch grace. These moments of grace are life-transforming. To be witness to them has been my deepest honour, for they stand testimony to the truth that out of the deepest caverns of darkness a bright light does shine. When we surrender our need to be right and place peace before all else, we can stand back and look with a much broader perspective not only at the history of our family, and therefore our own history, but also at the history of humanity, and gain a glimpse of purpose when we see the intricate workings of fate. I do not know if there is a key to fate, or some great conducting force that determines the twists of fate. The only thing I do know is that fate is our friend if we accept it and rise up to benefit from its gifts. We always have a choice.

Some things to remember:

- Fate is a given. It cannot be changed. Only our feelings about it can be changed.

- We inherited many of our beliefs from our parents and ancestors. These, too, can be changed.

- We often limit our lives out of loyalty to those who have suffered.

- Loyalty to those who have suffered neither serves them nor honours them.

- We create our experience and our reality according to the beliefs we hold. As we change our beliefs, we can change our reality.

- Feelings and beliefs are choices. No one ever forced any of them upon us. We either capitulated or simply accepted them without question.

- You are not here to become, or be, or do anything that is not who you truly are. Your mission is whatever you make of it.

- Gratitude is a major key to all healing processes.

- It is important to understand what is your business, what belongs to another, and what belongs to fate.

- The world does not need saving; it can take care of itself. We only need saving from ourselves.

Whether we only get one life or many, we may as well have some fun doing it. Enjoyment of life is all about choices. We can choose to focus on the negative, or choose to focus on all that is good, glorious, wonderful and beautiful about ourselves and the world.

L'Chaim – To Life!

About the Author

Author John L. Payne has spent his entire life traveling the world, living in such far-flung places as Australia, Africa, Europe and the Caribbean. His exposure to many cultures, languages and traditions has made him one of the most insightful teachers of our time, merging established western psychotherapeutic process with echoes of shamanism, as well as with traditional and spiritual healing.

John Payne currently offers Trans-Generational Healing and Family Constellations workshops worldwide in addition to his teachings on the Four Principles of Creation. He is glad to accept invitations to your city, town, state or country.

For more information regarding John's work, please visit his website, www.johnlpayne.com, or e-mail him directly at john@johnlpayne.com.

If you would like to gain more in-depth knowledge of generationally-transferred trauma, belief systems and feelings, we welcome you to explore John's earlier books on family constellations:

The Healing of Individuals, Families and Nations (2005)
The Language of the Soul (2006)

If you would like to gain more knowledge of The Four Principles of Creation and John Payne's work as a trance channel, please visit his alternative website, www.fourprinciples.com. We welcome you to explore John's first book on the Four Principles of Creation:

Omni Reveals the Four Principles of Creation.

The Four Principles of Creation

CD Selection

Together with Omni, John Payne has created a series of CD's that will elevate you to new levels of discovery and self-knowledge. Each CD is produced with the intention of giving you the tools to transform your life, let go of your limitations and fears, allowing you to move beyond what you currently know.

Omni Speaks – Live Recordings
- Introduction to the Four Principles of Creation
- Discovering Your Life's Purpose
- Manifesting with Joy
- Creating Abundance
- Higher Will & Reality Creation
- Inner Guidance
- Using Intention
- Keys to Happiness
- Sexuality
- Reincarnation, Karma & Belief Systems

Channeled Meditation Processes
- Attracting Your Soulmate
- The Art of Manifesting
- Healing Relationships
- Manifesting Your Life's Work – Vol 1
- Manifesting Your Life's Work – Vol 2
- Channeling Your Spirit Guide

New CDs will be produced on a regular basis

For on-line ordering, please visit www.fourprinciples.com
eMail enquiries to: info@fourprinciples.com

In the USA: 803-736-9240 (EST 9am – 5am)

FINDHORN PRESS

Books, Card Sets,
CDs & DVDs
that inspire and uplift

For a complete catalogue,
please contact:

Findhorn Press Ltd
305a The Park, Findhorn
Forres IV36 3TE
Scotland, UK

Telephone +44-(0)1309-690582
Fax +44-(0)1309-690036
eMail info@findhornpress.com

or consult our catalogue online
(with secure order facility) on
www.findhornpress.com